From Missouri to the Mojave

From Missouri to the Mojave

By Erma Peirson

with Robert Peirson

Copyright © 2025 by Robert Peirson
All rights reserved.
Illustrated by Robert Peirson

No part of this book may be reproduced in any form or by any electronic or mechanical means, including information storage and retrieval systems, without written permission from the author, except for the use of brief quotations in a book review.

ISBN: 979-8-9914131-5-2 (Hardback)
ISBN: 979-8-9914131-3-8 (Paperback)
ISBN: 979-8-9914131-4-5 (Ebook)

Dedicated to Professor Higgins and the Country School Teachers of the Bygone Era.

Table of Contents

Introduction 1

Chapter 1: Country School Teacher (1909) 5
    1890's Fashion 6
    New Eras 8
    Generations 10
    Ozark Hills 12
    Beloved Professor 15
    A Mother's Lantern 16
    Prohibition 17
    Conditions of a Bygone Era 18
    Another State and Another Certificate 20
    Hometown Reflections 22
    Moving Westward 28
    Nebraska Country Teacher 30

Chapter 2: My Tenderfoot Sister (1913) 33
    The Great Mojave Desert 34
    The Mojave River 36
    From Los Angeles to the Desert 36
    A New Home 37
    All Shining and Bright 39
    Cactus 43
    Desert Pets 45
    Master Painter 46
    Trips to Victorville 48
    The Kingdom of the Sun 49

Chapter 3: Lone Tree School (1919) 53
    Fallon, Nevada 55
    My New School 58
    The Flag 60
    Troubles 61
    Exhibit – Teaching Experience 64

Chapter 4: Bide A Wee Ranch (1922) 65
    Twenty Acres 66
    Little Castle 68
    Job Changes 71
    A New Addition 73
    End of a Dream 73

Chapter 5: Desert 'Scape (1943) 77
    We Come to the Desert 78
    The Spaces 85
    Patterns 90
    Mornings 100
    Sunsets 103

Chapter 6: Desert Fascinates (1948) 107

Chapter 7: Television: The One-Eyed Monster (1949) 111

Erma (Patterson) Peirson – Extended Biography 115

Introduction

In April 2008, I took a road trip with my dad, Bill Peirson, to visit the Grand Canyon. He was the youngest of three children and born to Erma and Wilfred Peirson. I am one of their twelve grandchildren. He grew up in the Mojave and has seen much of the desert from California to Arizona. But at the age of seventy-eight, he still had not been to the Grand Canyon. So, off we went on a father and son road trip.

One of the important stops along the way was to see the house in Barstow, CA, where he'd lived for two years in the early 1940s at the age of around thirteen years old. We drove up to the house just north of downtown, and it was still standing! Here is what he told me about the house:

"This is the house we lived in from 1943 to 1944 when we first moved to Barstow. They did a nice job fixing it up. Just Doris, Mom, Dad and I lived there. I had the run of the place. I was there all by myself for the entire summer. Doris had gotten a job. It was kind of nice when school started to have found some friends."

He went on to talk about the job his mom, Erma Peirson, had. "My mom would walk to work. She would walk down here to Highway 58. She got a job in Yermo, which is out that way (eastward). She'd walk down there in the morning and then sometimes she'd walk back at night. She would catch her bus right here (the corner of their street and Hwy 58) that took her to Yermo. The buses were all government buses. Sometimes she'd take them back from Yermo all the way to Barstow. Dad would drive into Barstow, and everybody would meet there and drive home."

In 2016, our father passed away at the age of eighty-six and so we moved our mom closer to where I live in Southern California. Among our parents' belongings were many boxes of family keepsakes. Among his papers, I found a box of our grandmother Erma's writings and research. It was like discovering a time capsule that contained newspaper articles and manuscripts that she had written during her lifetime.

Her obituary stated that she was working on a book about the history of Fresno at the time of her death in 1971. Thus, the first thing to research was a series of articles from the *Fresno Guide* called "Fresno's Past." My sister Susan, along with myself, assembled them into a book by the same name that we posthumously published in 2024. Erma Peirson had also published two earlier books, *Kern's Desert* (1956), and *The Mojave River and Its Valley* (1970).

From our review of her written material, we found the basis for a new book about Death Valley, which she had mentioned the desire to cover in an article, as well as expanded editions for her earlier subjects of the Kern Desert and Mojave River Valley. It is our endeavor to get these historic writings into the public view.

Nestled among her files were multiple autobiographical manuscripts where she reflected on her life. These were written from the mid-1940s to the mid-1950s during which time she became an empty nester as her children, one by one, moved out of her home to begin their professional lives.

I would like to thank my sister, Susan (Peirson) Bates, for all of her involvement in this family project, including helping transcribe the typed and her manuscript proofreading. In addition, I would like to thank my cousin and great grandson of Erma, James Colannino, for his proofreading assistance.

A special thank you to the Churchill County Museum of Fallon, NV and the Plainsman Museum of Aurora, NE for their research help and photographic contributions.

I am pleased to offer these stories of her early life in Missouri, Nebraska, Central California, Nevada, and the Mojave Desert.

Enjoy.

Robert Peirson, 2025
Grandson of the author, Erma Peirson

Introduction

My father, Bill Peirson, in front of his childhood house in Barstow, CA during a visit in 2008. The front porch along with the addition in the back had been added along with other upgrades. High athel trees that were there in 1943 can be seen to the left. (photo by Robert Peirson)

Chapter 1
Country School Teacher (1909)

Written in the late-1950s, these are personal reflections of Erma's time as a Country School Student in St. Clair County, Missouri. She lived with her parents, George and Martha Patterson, her older sister Ruby and younger sister Almeda. Included are her thoughts on early school ages to 1908 graduation, 1909 teacher training and then moving to Nebraska after her father passed away.

My 1908 graduation picture from High School in Osceola, St. Clair County, Missouri

I, who was the dreamy child of the quaint desire, ran the gauntlet of life with all the little girls of my day. We wore pigtails, not as the fad of today with only a few favoring the hair dress, but pigtails for convenience and common sense. They were an invitation to the boys who loved to sneak up behind the girls and yank the tresses. But curls on Sunday, my, yes! Whether they were natural or manufactured from the long kid-wrapped wire curlers or the long, narrow rags like those used for making rugs and carpets, curls were for Sunday, parties, and for special school occasions. Calico dresses for play and for the warmer months of school, heavy woolen ones for winter. Much betucked and insertioned and ruffled dresses for Sunday-go-to-meeting. No colorful sun suits or sun dresses for the small-town gals of that day nor skirts or pleated dresses. Long, black stockings (for those that didn't go barefooted) for play hours. Long, white stockings for dress up occasions. Never a "bobby sock", "half sock", or "short sock". And only very well-to-do papas bought silk stockings (they weren't called hose in that era) for their daughters, only possibly for Christmas gifts or very special birthdays.

1890s Fashion

Rayon was an unknown quantity, and nylon as a word would have made a Websterian of that time gasp. High-top shoes for "every day", and low-cut shoes, called slippers for rest. Sandals, so popular in this modern age, were for monks and friars and for Oriental people. A toeless shoe would have been a sign of degeneracy.

How could a child of that day have been shoe conscious, anyway? With their mothers, the teachers, and all grown-up ladies wearing dresses to the floor. When one thinks of feet in those times, and now! Of the styles then compared to those of today, not only in footwear but in all phases of apparel. When this bewildered dreamer began her schooling, all one could see of a lady's foot was a pointed toe, a sensible heel and perhaps a foot—no, two feet—of latticed shoestring, or possibly an ankle length row of beady, bird's-eye buttons.

Country School Teacher (1909)

Those high shoes, in various patterns, continued for many years after 'Small Feet' began to teach her own schools in the 'Nineteen Twenties'.

The modern shoe plays a great part in life today, not only for style but for health. Sometimes it is the tapering, toothpick heel, or the toeless shoe, open heel, wedge heels or flat heels, but all are scaled to mold a healthy foot. The long brown legs are much in evidence with no shame attached. Silk or something synthetic may cover the healthy length, but there is no false modesty about the legs, be they shapely or otherwise.

Smart? Of course. The most sedate teacher, or any woman left over from the lavender and lace halo that lingers like a lovely memory to us of the 'Nineties, regardless of age, will allow that much for modern dress, and follow their stride. My little friends and sisters ran unhobbled, climbed trees, and otherwise had themselves quite a childhood, foot free, shoe loose, during the summer months in the Ozark foothills. I lived to see my two dreams materialize, but the hard way. The one, not because I went barefooted, I'm sure, but because nature endowed me with a small-boned body; the other because not only was teaching a serious dream for me, but it was one of the few vocations for a small-town girl ten years past the present century.

Back in the 'Sixteen Hundreds' a wag, named Colley Cibber said, "As good be out of the world as out of fashion." So the world keeps step with the styles through the generations, both men and women. I can remember when boys in high school still wore knee pants and long black stockings. What a chore their mothers had during marble time.

Along with the freedom of today's styles, we have forgotten that the lower extremities ever caused embarrassment when spoken of as legs. That is another sign of progress with the years.

The long dresses spoken of have not gone out of vogue. Long dresses are still worn, but they are for evening, or lounging, or hostess occasions. Worn long for grace and beauty, not for reasons of modesty.

Can we not remember vividly, us oldsters, hearing how terrible it was to see a "leg show"? Remember the gag of the baldheaded row? Also, how dreadful was it then to have one's daughter go "on the stage"? Not only was it a dreadful thing because of one's morals, but because the gayety roles called for showing the legs. Oh, Betty Grable, where were you?

The freedom of the times! But in that past day when I, the solemn-visaged dreamer, went to school, we saw little of a lady's foot. Years later when I stood before my first pupils on my own two uncertain feet that somehow had kept up with the rest of me, ladies' dresses were fast reaching the shoe-top length (of high shoes). Before my teaching career was to end, dresses went up to the knees, and I don't mean below the knees.

We've come a long way in styles. Somehow, morals haven't suffered too much.

New Eras

There is no need here to rave over much about the times and morals, but this volume is planned in part to record the passing of old viewpoints along with the passing of the little red schoolhouse of that other day.

What we love today belongs to us today. What we loved of another day belongs to us in memory.

We face new eras quite frequently in these later years. Possibly it all means progress. These eras are not distinguished by calendar years, but by the whims of inventions and desires. There have been times I have viewed with great alarm the record-breaking crises of the world. Each war I have lived through has brought many changes. Sometimes I wonder what yet will face my grandchildren and my unborn grandchildren. There is a faint memory of the Spanish American War, either from remembrance of talk in the home, or reminiscing from my elders later. World War I is very vivid to me, yet as my cousins and friends went off to war. I've seen one son through a World War and the other through the Korean "police action". The Holocausts have done much to change the times and the morals and education.

I, who remember maps hung from the top of blackboards many years ago, and who later taught year in and year out by rote what I had learned about the countries of the hemisphere, and could name countries and their capitals, wonder when the maps will have changed for the last time, and if the world will return to the even keel we enjoyed before world wars disrupted us.

We have progressed far though, even considering wars. What with sciences and inventions of things once thought fantastical, there is "never a dull moment in life."

I am reminded here of "Mother Shipton's" prophecy. I remember hearing of it, and reading it, many years ago. It is said to have been written about 1510 by "Mother Shipton," who must indeed have had a vision of "things to come". I quote:

> When pictures look alive with movements free,
> When ships, like fishes, swim below the sea,
> When men, outstripping birds, can scour the sky,
> Then half the world, deep-drenched in blood, shall die.

I think we have progressed with sandals and sun suits, shorts, trunks, and halters. Look what happened in Los Angeles back in 1940.

An adventurous news reporter decided to roam the streets downtown clad only in an ultra-brief pair of shorts to see if the populace would rise up in arms. He spent most of the day purposely putting himself in other people's paths in order "to get a rise" out of somebody for appearing on the streets sans any conventional clothing (except the abbreviated shorts). Even his friend, the insurance salesman whom he encountered, disregarded his apparel and started trying to sell a policy. Not a lady as much as turned her head toward or away from him. Not a child but what took it in its stride, taking for granted that an adult had the same rights as he did when he donned his bathing trunks for a shower bath in the backyard. Streetcar conductors ignored the unusual garb, intent only upon securing fare. Nor did the policeman, under whose official nose the reporter thrust his appearance by asking directions, give him a thought other than nonchalantly pointing out the way.

Yes, of course, that happened in Los Angeles. But had that happened in Los Angeles in the 1910s, what a different tale that reporter would have had to turn in to his city editor.

Oh, the times. Oh, the lack of morals!

Generations of Patterson Women. From the left, sister Almeda Patterson, myself Erma Patterson, mother Martha (Marlow) Patterson, sister Ruby Patterson and grandmother Almira (Palmer) Marlow.

Generations

Step by step through the years I took life in stride as I lived in my beloved Missouri hills. I can remember my mother's bustle, the long trailing dresses she wore for street and formal calls. I recall the silk mitts and the lacy parasol. I'm intrigued now as I look at pictures of her with her lovely black curly hair, smartly done in the coiffure of the moment. I know, despite the natural wave, that she used the old fashioned "curling iron" even as I did in my teens and later years. But she never had a permanent in her life. She was among the first to have her hair bobbed, and in all the years since the curling-iron period—and long before—she wore her hair in natural waves, capped down to her head in back, beautiful yet when she went to rest in her eighty-sixth year.

Her daughters came down the years with the changing styles of hair dress, trying out the fads and fancies. Even as my daughter has done since her Shirley Temple days, when I wound some sixty-odd curls over my fingers daily. I loved watching this daughter as she grew up. She had the grace of a fawn, and she went barefooted, even riding her bicycle without shoes when it suited her whim and convenience. She was never hampered by petticoats as I was. Well, I remember the numerous petticoats my mother swaddled me in. I also remember along in our early teens, my sisters and I would slip some of them off on the way to Sunday school, hide them under a bridge or bushes so we would be less hampered in our stride, go merrily on, picking them up on the way home. Just as we wore our sunbonnets hanging down our backs instead of on our heads. By the time my young lady came on the scene, the word petticoat was going into discard. The name is now "slip". This daughter was no pale faced one to faint at a whim as legend tells us the belles of her grandmother's day did. And her feet were always out of proportion to the rest of her. And she wanted to be a teacher!

With her contemporaries she wore shorts and halters and slacks and pedal pushers, all of which were never heard of in my youthful days. The mere thought of such garments would have made us blush for shame. She has jitterbugged, but her morals have not suffered. She is a part of the new destiny. We must admit there is a lot of common sense in the changing trends in clothes.

I am reminded of an old jingle song I used to hear from the first phonograph records I ever listened to. The meat of the lyric was,

"They've left us our old blue jean pants and we ought to be thankful for that." The resigned author of the verses and those men folks who sang them sincerely are probably turning over in the graves at the fate of the blue jeans.

This is as good a place as any other to speak of the progress of the phonograph. What excitement there was when the first phonograph made its appearance in the small towns and countryside areas. Groups would gather and stand awed as the music and words poured out of the monstrous horn placed atop the box, small and out of proportion to the horn, that held the mechanism that ground out the sound to the listening groups. What if it was wheezy, scratchy, and tinny. It was progress. How far afield we have come with our radios, television, and of course, the par excellence phonographs.

Although the desire and ambition to be a schoolteacher seemed to start long before I realized what it meant, in time there came a burning desire to "teach the young idea how to shoot."

Ozark Hills

One of the things I have looked forward to for many, many years is a trip back to that little town in the Ozark Hills, mainly to see if the old Madison house is still standing. Regardless of if it has gone with time and tide, it would not matter because it has lived in my memory for as long as I can remember. It must have made a deep impression on my small girl mind, for even yet, whenever I read a story, the setting is mentally placed in the same house. The house in the story may be small, medium, or castle-like. The memory expands to fit the story. Should there be a detailed description of the setting? Somehow it becomes evolved into a two-story Madison house with the pond, the maple trees, and the cornfield where we youngsters played and where we gathered silks from the ears of corn to use for tresses on our homemade dolls. This same cornfield helped to produce "shuck hats," which were quite fetching and were really worn. The smoothed-out husks were woven and plaited to form brims and crowns.

Country School Teacher (1909)

Among the many "Missouri" stories my mother often related was of a native of these parts. At a gathering one time, a church social, perhaps, or at a picnic, someone's proper pronunciation of the word "potatoes" was challenged by another lady in the group. "My goodness", she drawled, "Mary Jane always did call taters potatoes!" Mother got a "kick out" of observations of human nature wherever she went.

And it was the same when my folks went down to the hills of Missouri from the sandhills of Nebraska. They found some of the customs and some of the colloquialisms different than they had been used to in Nebraska, Illinois, Wisconsin and back in my father's "York State." One particular phrase mixed them up for a time until they "tumbled" and probably followed suit. It was the habit of calling anything after noon "evening". My father couldn't understand why, when he showed up at nightfall to fulfill an engagement made, that he found no one, and was later, to the puzzlement of his New York soul, told the engagement was for a time after "dinner", the noon hour.

During a portion of our elementary-high school years, 1896-1909, we read with interest the popular children's books of the times. We were somewhat familiar with the (Horatio) Alger series for boys along with *Robinson Crusoe* by Daniel Defoe. We cried heartbreakingly over the stories of Black Beauty, the story horse, and Beautiful Joe, the dog. We lived eagerly the lives of the *Little Women* in Louisa M. Alcott's series, and we shared our heart throbs for Elsie Dinsmore and her perfection and the burning characters in *Uncle Tom's Cabin*.

It is also a part of that childhood memory of the funnies of the day. The skits were not thought of as "comics"; that was to come later. But we lived weekly with the Katzenjammer Kids.

We went adventuring with the Swiss Family Robinson people and into Treasure Island, and we loved the good that Robin Hood did.

These titles are only a few of the rich story—a heritage we fell heir to. We are quite sure, we of that past era, that the books did us no harm. Many a boy came to the top in the world because of ambitions alerted by reading the Alger books, and many a girl was better spiritually because of Elsie Dinsmore, even though her life would seem pretty pale to the approaching teenagers today.

I have wondered what has become of the enchanting tradition of hanging May baskets on the eve of May Day. Perhaps the May Pole dances and programs in the schools have taken the place of that charming annual project. How we worked for days on end to fashion a variety of paper May baskets, filled them with spring flowers and ran at dusk to hang them on the doors for our favorite friends. If there happened to be a doorbell, the clear tones announcing someone at the door was the signal to scamper out of sight. If there were no bell, a rap was the custom. I remember particularly one man who was what was later termed a grouch. He had a couple of small daughters, delightfully doll-like. When we went to this house the first time, he became angered at the "botheration"; later, someone, an adult, went to the house and explained the May basket idea. To his credit, he was kinder to the later ones who left their fragrant offerings.

Beloved Professor

We appreciated you, Professor, with that thin, angular body as you stood before us for the last time. I can see yet the long, relaxed arms as you walked to the center of the old opera house stage to make an address. Impressed forever were the contortions of your face during the last remarks as you tried in your manliness and scholastic dignity to keep back the tears that fell every May when you graduated a class.

Oh, dearly beloved 'Fessor', as we called you, I hope you will be able to read these words before your years run out. And when, and if you do, be it known now to you that your patience, your great heart, and the sincere love you felt for us has never been forgotten. You had no consolidated school to preside over; no special departments; no playground apparatus; no expert instructors; but you had a heart.

Country School Teacher (1909)

1908 graduating class picture from high school, Osceola, St. Clair County, Missouri. Seated is Professor Higgins. My sister Ruby Patterson is seated with my hand on her shoulder. Far right is Eva Wheller and far left is Mary Lewis.

You could laugh with us at the little mouse who came out and stood on its small haunches beside the woodpile that cluttered up a corner of the larger high school room. You could understand the pranks and giggles as well as the ambitions of those under your guidance.

Out of this class of seven that 'Fessor' graduated that year were five girls. Two of us became teachers, a plump, jolly girl named Mary, and me and my feet. Mary, a grandmother, is still teaching, up in Montana. We were not destined to teach the year following our graduation. For that was the time when the district added the fourth year to our high school. Several of us returned for that extra, helpful year.

It was one more year of companionship with the friends in the grades below us, one more year of the good professor's direction, a much surer forging ahead with the added knowledge. A little more mathematics was ground into the head who had no thought or love for figures.

It was wise, that extra year, for, still discouraging the freckles, I was one of thousands and thousands who stood in 1909 getting her bearings to enter the field of employment. To be eighteen and ready to take over a school of one's own was a momentous event. College was not in the picture for me that year. And somehow, it never was. I suppose one would say I came up the hard way.

A Mother's Lantern

We paraded to the hen house by the light of my mother's lantern. My mother's lantern, let me say in an aside, was a legend in our little town. She was always so anxious for our safety that when we went anywhere unchaperoned by an adult, Mother came after us, guided by the feeble glow of her swinging lantern. Mother, a comely woman of forty, must have felt herself immune to the onslaughts of the feared disasters. In our town, we had a constant fear of the colored people, many of whom lived in "Sleepy Hollow." Not all of them, but we quite feared the men in one family. In those days, we had no 'wolves' to worry about. It was unadulterated fear. But like the mother of any animal, she had no fear where her young were concerned.

But, I was out of debt. I was a full-fledged, certified teacher to be. The professor was as thrilled as I. I do not even have to close my eyes to see us after more than forty years. A nostalgia floods me. My mother, stout and jolly, like a female Diogenes, preceded us down the lily-of-the-valley bordered path, through the vegetable garden, past the barn where the mill horses neighed to us, and where the old red cow chewed her eternal cud, to the weather-beaten hen house. Our gentle friend and neighbor followed with the gunny sacks, my sisters and me in tow.

In memory, the sloping yard lies silver in the moonlight that came spreading over the quiet world. I feel the softness of the night around me, and I hear the squawking of the chickens who resented the intrusion upon their slumbers. There is still the thrill of being launched. When the children bring home their grades and awards from universities, neither their thrills nor mine are any greater than rested upon my slender form as someone held high my mother's lantern in the darkness of the hen house.

Dear Professor, whatever these pages tell of success or failure, for the understandings of the comings and goings of life about me, know that only of the better things you had a part. Know that, as I have taught in the intervening years since we filed out of the henhouse when my mother handed over to you her chickens as payment for my first "professional" training as a teacher and your efforts to make of me something I admired in you, that have tried never to disappoint.

We had no special graduation exercises for the eighth grade or junior high school. Our goal, a great moment in life, was high school finishing.

Prohibition

No picture of those late Nineties and early Nineteen Hundreds would be complete without a glimpse of a "blind tiger." Prohibition, while not always so-called, was a bone of contention. Like all frustrations, this phase brought about law violations. If a saloon was closed, it would be just as easy to procure liquor as it was in the later days of the speakeasies. Usually, these blind tigers were seated in the small-town drug stores.

This was the era of the country churches, too. Wagons, buggies, and carts were modes of transportation. The edifices stood still and solemn on village street corners, or out on country roads, usually painted white, standing out as things apart. Here people came for devotional richness, possibly knowing their Bible lore as well as the ministers did, but happily listening to him preach about their sins and their dalliances for eternal life. The youth of the day flocked to the little churches. Except for the community life that centered in school houses, much of one's life emanated from the small churches. Those who accepted the denominational or devotional messages came for enjoyment; those who sought balm in Gilead came to the solemn walls; those who sought advice, or God, or a way of life, filled the room. The youth came, seeking companionship.

Usually in these little churches, and the high schools as well, music was furnished by old-fashioned organs. Pianos were not so commonly used. Well-fixed homes, too, boasted an organ. They were wonderful creations, really seeming more intricate than the more expensive pianos. Community music played a great part in the rural homes in that far away time before the radio and television became accepted phases of life. We must not forget to recall the old type of phonograph with its great horn.

We would not want to erase the memory of the corn husking bees, the building get-togethers, the quilting bees, the church suppers, the watermelon feeds and swipes.

The little buildings—the schools, the churches, the homes, the crossroads stores—each has contributed something to the present age, even as the "hand that rocks the cradle rules the world". The influence of those days is felt now. It has all been a part of the plan for progress of a great nation. It may have started on the Atlantic seaboard; in the Ohio wildernesses; the Tennessee mountains; the Ozark foothills; the Nebraska prairies; the western plains and mountains; the denseness of the Northwest, or the deserts of the Southwest.

Conditions of a Bygone Era

In these small places we fought the battles of germs and diseases, sometimes losing the battles. In some places the only method of fighting flies was the constant fanning of tree branches over a dinner table. Screens at doors and windows were often never seen in some of the country places in the Missouri hills where I have spent a day. How well I recall the sickening sight of the old flypaper, which held a sticky substance spread over the surface. We bought them by the sheets. The flies, attracted to the sweetish odor, made unhappy landings. Often it was necessary to use these even in homes protected by screens.

Country School Teacher (1909)

The fly problem was almost as hard to lick as the tainted well water. Many homes had as standing fixtures the cisterns where water was accumulated from rainfall and brought up by the "old oaken bucket", or hand pump. In many places, of course, the water comes from natural sources. These cisterns (as well as the uncovered wells) took the lives of many, mostly children, when they were left uncovered.

The little red schoolhouse is on its way out. It has been for many years. It is about to vanish. Sometimes the country school buildings were white. Sometimes drab and unpainted. In some places they were made of logs. A statistic records that in 1952 there are less than 70,000 one-room country schools. Almost a dozen a day are going out of existence. Seventy thousand sounds like a big figure, but compare that with the 200,000 one roomers back in 1916 and estimate how many will be left some 36 years from now.

Get a picture of the children traipsing to school, a mile, two, or three miles, carrying dinner pails, usually a bucket that once held lard filled with cold food. But, they thrived. How many would do that now in these days of buses and consolidated schools? The fact of the matter is that they accepted the situation as a part of their mode of life.

```
U. S. POST OFFICE.
E. E. BUZZARD, Post Master.
J. TAYLOR, Ass't P. M.

                                Collins, Mo.,   May 7th '09.
Miss Erma Patterson,
         I am enclosing you your papers.   As I telephoned your
mother yesterday you have been given a place in the school here.
You and Miss Eckla McFall have been selected for the two lower rooms
but we did not decide which should have the primary and which the
intermediate.      However it is my opinion that you will be given
the primary and Miss McFall the intermediate if that is agreeable
to both of you and I presume it will be.   This however is only
my opinion and it is not worth any more than any one else's Opinion.
I trust both of you young teachers will prove to be good teachers
and make good educators.   Come down to see us when you can.
                                Very truly yours,
                                          E. E. BUZZARD.
```

Acceptance to begin my teaching career in Collins, Missouri where I later had to resign.

Another State and Another Certificate

When September 1909 dawned in Missouri, there were no school bells for me. Late in August my father passed away at the age of only

54 years old. He had been ill for so very long. He had pneumonia in the winter before and had never been well again. Although there were no effects from the pneumonia that bothered him, the doctors said. But the siege had weakened his system. Today, the pneumonia would have been checked immediately by the wonder drugs we have. Then, he just had to see it through, get well or die, at home. He had the best of care, but there were no hospitals there. We were so far from cities where specialists practiced. But I do remember our family physician, who as all old-time family physicians were, was a family friend, too, brought in a specialist from Kansas City. But there was nothing to do for him. It seemed there was some spinal trouble.

My father was a good man. There was never a time when he did not go down into his pockets to help for charity or to help feed a needed citizen or friend. But he was never what one would call a religious man, if going to church is the definition for a religious person. He belonged to fraternal organizations and was honored in them. I never saw my father in a church. It was the mother who kept us on that straight and narrow path. I know it must have been a great burden on my good Baptist mother to know that her husband, and the father of her children, was outside of the church. I never knew if she tried to convert him to being a Christian or not. She was never a meddler. She took what came to her, the good and the bad. She enjoyed the good and prayed over the bad. She must have done a great deal of praying over the fact that my father was unprepared to meet his Maker. And it was a wonderful day for her during the last weeks of that wretched summer when he asked to have our professor come to see him. Professor came and sat with him alone for a long time. Later, my father told my mother he "had made his peace with his Lord." He died soon after. I never knew why he did not call a minister. But he trusted and liked our pedagogue.

A new life was ahead of us. For some reason my Mother did not want to stay in Missouri. So, we planned to go to Nebraska, her former state and where all her people lived. I don't believe that even the adventure of a new place made us girls eager to go. We were so happy in our little hill town. I don't believe for a minute that Mother thought she was doing us an injustice by moving. I'm sure she thought it was for the best and that we would have advantages in the new country.

My older sister gave up her position as typesetter in one of the weekly newspaper offices and went on ahead to Nebraska with the body of our father after the large funeral, which was held at our home, and which overflowed into the yard. Relatives had come down from the prairie state to be with us before my father passed away and they accompanied her. The church of our mother and us girls gave my father his funeral. His Masonic lodge buried him in Nebraska.

It was hard to leave what had been our home for so many years. Where our hearts had been impressed; where our youthful good times had been so pleasant.

I resigned from my school. All my borrowed finery and my forcing myself to look and act so aged were now a memory to be relegated to the past. I have often wondered why I did not stay and teach that year. I remember a good friend, whom we affectionately called Uncle Charley, editor of the *Democrat*, the paper where my sister worked, scolded me roundly, but gently, because I broke my contract. But what was I to do? My mother wanted to go back to her people and wanted, in her new, unsettled world, her girls with her. She didn't want to leave me behind. I never quite figured out why it was worse for the school board to find another teacher than it was for Uncle Charley to find another typesetter.

We sold our home to the good professor. He had the rambling white structure. He would sit in the library to grade papers and talk with students, where my father had sat for endless evenings reading every history, profane and sacred, that he could lay his hands on, and of which he never forgot a word with that remarkable memory of his that had helped him so much in his mechanics and mathematics. The beloved professor and his family would enjoy the vast green lawn, the shady oaks and maple trees we had loved. The lilies of the valley, which bordered the paths around the place, and which have stayed in my memory through the years, becoming my favorite flower, were left to the kindly ministrations of my favorite educator and his several small children who would run through Mother's garden, and his wife would harvest the fruit and vegetables, and store them in preserved state in her treasured cellar. He would have our hen house and bring our chickens literally home to roost.

Hometown Reflections

We were leaving the rocks and hills; the gleaming Osage river where we had sailed in the "Osceola", the first motorboat on the river. Of course that would belong to my father, leading mechanic of the area. The flour mill would be in other hands. Old Sam Barker, a Civil War veteran with his one lung, would take back his old gray horse and no longer be teamster for my father. His Shepherd dog, which for some obscure reason was named "Pug," was given to my older sister. Ruby often rode the horses, and "Pug" always followed her. "Pug" was to go to Nebraska.

We were leaving. The City of the Seven Hills, where my childhood's happiest days had been spent, and which has always been "my hometown", was soon to be in my past.

A memory, the little white church where we sat every Sunday morning and evening, listening to a variety of ministers of the old-time religion of hell-fire and brimstone, which would find another organist than my sister. Others would continue to search for the Indian arrowheads around about. We wouldn't dart in anymore at the boarding house run by Miss Jess Williams, who is still today a landmark of the old town and listen to talks about the Mason-Dixon line, which ran through the town, and which, back in 1909, was still a sore topic of conversation among the elders.

"Sleepy Hollow" and its colored population would go on being run out by the spring floods that backed into town from old Gallinipper Creek, a tributary of the Osage. We'd never got to witness another move of old Aunt Vine, the aged and almost mountainous

Country School Teacher (1909)

colored woman who sat in front of her shanty and smoked a pipe, who moved to higher ground each spring.

The Debate Team, 1908-09, from left to right, Mary Lewis, myself Erma Patterson, Helen Conant and Ruth Ebbs.

There would be no more trips in the fall after nuts and berries and grapes. No more possum hunts at the old Love Farm a mile or so from town, where the town youngsters always loved to go. The Love Farm was owned by a Baptist minister. What a busy place it was. It was a treat to go out there on a Saturday and follow my pal, Ruth, around. Ruth, one of the pastor's several daughters, was in my second graduating class and one of the most worthwhile girls I ever knew. Large physically, she was mentally what today the kids would call a "brain." We used to marvel at her. Sometimes we envied her farm life. Again, we pitied her. We used to marvel at the vast amount of work that girl did before she got to school at nine o'clock in the morning. I can't remember the number of cows she milked twice a day. And she never missed a day of school, nor much of the fun. Of course, as I look back, I know lots of our fun emanated from her home, where in the old-fashioned parlor, long and narrow, with austere furnishings, the stereoscope lay with its hundreds of double picture cards, which when brought up to the eye like a huge two-dimensioned goggle, produced one large scene. There was always a definite reality to the pictures thus seen. Old "Brother Love," who was so strict with his large family, at least provided well for their culture. Of the five girls of his second wife, which I recall so vividly, so patient, hard-working and such a wonderful mother, they all had their schooling and became schoolteachers. There was a grand (and large) family before the one I knew.

No more could I walk over to the lovely home of Thomas Moore Johnson that stood like a colonial mansion near the banks of the river and browse through the large library that belonged to this well-known Latin, Hebrew, and Greek student. Moore Johnson was one of our most well-known men, and what I would class as a number one citizen. He was a small man, slender and deep-eyed, by far the best educated man that we had ever had in our small community. Adjoining his spacious and palatial home was a small cottage of four rooms where he spent most of his waking hours. The four rooms were literally lined from floor to ceiling, except where windows and doors were placed, with books. We had no public library. The only library other than Mr. Johnson's I had ever seen was the one the Class of 1908 started in a small room just below the belfry at school. We all (the seven of us) donated a book or two each; thus the high school library started.

Country School Teacher (1909)

Thomas Moore Johnson graduated from Notre Dame and in 1873 had a law office in Nevada but after a short while, returned to his hometown of Osceola, Missouri where he would spend his life and focus on his study of philosophy. He was known for his published book *The Platonist* and was often referred as "The Sage of the Osage" and the "Missouri Platonist". (Kansas City Star, March 3, 1919)

We were very proud of our bookish townsmen. Among his most valued books was a Bible printed during the Fourteen Hundreds. Many were the books this good man loaned me. He was so ready to do anything that would foster education. Debating was one of my "long suits" when I was in high school. Whatever the subject that came up, and whichever side I happened to advocate, I could always get material by browsing through his wonderful library.

He was a translator. It was Moore Johnson's habit to annually offer a five-dollar cash prize (no mean sum at the beginning of the century) for the best Latin student. It was a matter of translating. I've forgotten if we translated Latin to English or vice versa. All I know is I earned one of those prized five dollars, which came to me enclosed in a letter on his interesting stationery with a lot of words printed in Latin and Greek on the margins. Thomas Moore Johnson contributed a lot to the culture of our little town.

The Johnsons had three sons and a daughter. They were all well educated people and have become educators and lawyers. His wife was a busy clubwoman. The youngest son I must record because he put me in a quandary once. This son, the youngest in his class, was called Pete, though his first name was Frank. He was a very advanced student. Pete graduated from the four-year high school course when he was thirteen years old. It was almost unheard of by anyone in a day of no quiz kids and few prodigies. We used to pity poor Pete because he studied so hard. What few of us realized at the time was that Pete didn't need any pity. He was really a brain, and he probably studied as hard and as long as he did because he wanted to. But the kids all felt it was because he was his father's son, and we looked for another Thomas Moore Johnson someday. He was a quiet, small boy, seldom having much to say to anyone. We thought it was shyness. Maybe it was, but it was probably because we were all so much inferior that we couldn't speak his language, and I'm not poking fun at him.

When graduation night came, I, along with a few others who were back for the second diploma which would give us a full four-year high school credit, had only to step onto the stage and receive the diplomas. We didn't have to sit there all evening and wait for the kind professor's tears. So, Pete's father asked me to hold the paper that recorded Pete's talk (he was, of course, valedictorian). Me, I was so proud to do something for so distinguished a man that I accepted

Country School Teacher (1909)

eagerly and stood in the wings with the paper in my hands to "correct" or "prompt" him. Not that I thought for a minute that Pete would forget a word. It wasn't in the cards for a Johnson to slip for want of a word. What I didn't count on was Pete's ingenuity and his individuality. Pete walked to the center of the stage to give his talk, a gesture of honor because of his high standard class work.

Pete went right along, talking in his soft voice, never faltering. But soon I couldn't find where "he was". I was quite bewildered. What if he faltered? How could I ever prompt him, if I couldn't find "the place"? It took me some very confusing moments to understand that Pete was very versatile. Pete was saying everything that was on the paper that he had originally composed and written, but Pete was unorthodoxly putting it in different words. The full extent of his "smartness" penetrated into my wondering, slow-thinking brain. Pete was really talking, not just parrot-like giving his prepared theme. He hadn't memorized it! He was not ad-libbing! He was saying something he knew something about. Knew it so well he didn't need to memorize it. Just as though he were talking to someone on a familiar subject, he spoke the words that evolved from his present moment of thought. I laid the paper aside. I doubt if he ever reclaimed it. I'd give a lot to remember what Pete's subject was. I'll ask him some day when I go back to the hills of old Missouri. I've heard through the grapevine of old school friends that he teaches in a college in Springfield. And to think we ever felt sorry for him!

[Editor's Note: Franklin Plotinos Johnson, AKA Pete, in 1919 was bequeathed by his father, Thomas Moore Johnson, the Johnson Library and stone building that holds it.]

Many of my friends were leaving for college. Those who did not went right into teaching or some other work. A substitute was found for my "room" at Collins. She taught there a few years and married someone. She met her "Fate" sooner than I did! Glover, the doctor's son, went away to take the prep course in medicine that he never completed. The dancing girl had gone to Kansas City. A pretty girl who had the loveliest hands we had ever seen, so white and well-formed and plump, married the son of one of the editors.

Moving Westward

Something of the vigor and thrill, the adventure and love of pioneer days, must surely have been bred in me, for I still quiver as I did when I was young at the thought of the wide-open spaces, great expanses of blue skies, low hills, a tree or two, and a one-roomed shack. The story *The Virginian* fell into my teenage hands and the recorded lure and adventures of the Great West set my imaginative mind traveling over the gulf of miles so that I wanted to live the life of a cowgirl. To make the West more fascinating to us, my chums, my sister, and myself, as well as several of the hometown boys had "gone West" and were cowboys in Wyoming and Montana. Their letters home were adventures for us. And later, there was the "Covered Wagon" to read.

Going to Nebraska wasn't the wild and woolly west by any means, but it had something for us to think about. At least it was nearer than Missouri to western romance. At least if we rode horseback, we could ride man-fashion. But when we reached Nebraska, we found no cowboys and no gun smoke. All the horses we saw were our uncles' old plow horses and the prancing steeds; the swains drove before their rubber-tired buggies. We weren't far enough westward to be in cattle country.

It was October 1909 before Mother and I left Missouri. There was an ache that day when we took the train. I was leaving so much. My schoolmates. My dear friend, the professor. The old brick schoolhouse where I had dreamed my dreams. The gorgeously colored wooded hills in autumn. The winding, silver, treacherous river that ran against the heart of Main Street.

There was the same sadness in the heart that was in the air of autumn. Blue skies were growing darker as the winter days advanced. The white clouds were not so feathery, but were massed, lying low in the heavens. With the heavier frost that was not too far distant, every tree in that little city of hills and every bush and tree on the riverbanks would take on a final triumph of color. Maple, oak, persimmon, haws, catalpa, sycamore and elm, and all the domestic fruit trees already flared forth in gold and tan, orange and many hues of brown, while all the earth beneath crackled as the leaves settled to form a stiff Persian pattern, and all the world above sighed in gentle winds.

With the house turned over to the professor's family, a happy feeling warmed us knowing that the walls would enfold a family we loved. We set forth westward.

We had studied freight rates and decided to take the furniture with us. We had intended to sell the cow, but found that if we took her, we could charter a car for livestock and could put the furniture in one end, the cow in the other. Mother, with an eye for business, purchased a large amount of coal, knowing that coal was more expensive in Nebraska than in Missouri where there were many coal mines. After the coal was loaded, she was informed that coal was not included in the price given for household goods and family livestock. So, the coal was unloaded. It was just as well, too, for after we reached Nebraska, we used a different kind of stove which called for "hard" coal.

One of my farmer cousins came down to go back with the freight car to look after old Jumper, the cow, and Pug, Ruby's dog.

After a short visit in Kansas City, where the mother, the little sister, and myself were exposed to diphtheria, we were again on our way.

The hills, in their ruddy autumn coloring, were soon gone, as were the deep gulches and rocky boulders. The train ran noticeably smoother, it seemed to us, which may have been our imagination. It was late October, and the skies were a beautiful blue. "October's bright blue weather" seems to be beautifully the same wherever one may go, just as June's "rare day." But there was a dearth of trees as we sped over the countryside. The towns had their quotas of elms and maples, and now and then a cherry orchard, but the denseness of trees was missing.

Up through the state Capitol, and forty miles westward, and then we were at our destination. New scenes. New people. New hopes. It was quite a change for us of the rugged country. We took rides about the country in the wagons and buggies. Automobiles were not so common then, but there were more than we had seen in our little hill community. There was scarcely a jolt there on the level prairie roads. Mother never, as long as she lived, or wherever she lived, got tired of talking about how the great grain wagons went over the miles, loaded to the rim of the high wagon beds, and not a grain was lost.

Nebraska Country Teacher

My uncle worked for my mother. He made a good man to take over the fine farm, and he added farm land of his own later. He was good to the boys, one of whom farmed with him. The other went to business school but in later years also farmed.

The great day was about to dawn for the first day of school. The mother had made new clothes for the teacher. A few books had been bought. An alarm clock was obtained for this country girl to get up in country hours, for one had to eat an early breakfast along with the farm hands, as that was the day when farmers were farmers, and there was a mile and a half to walk to open the school, see that it was warm during the winter, aired in the warmer months, and to get the school work lined up.

I thought it was fine that I was to live with my uncle's family. There were two to go to school from there. My little cousin of five (the legal school age in Nebraska for first grade.) And my 12- or 13-year-old cousin who was taking the eighth grade for the second time. The lad was bright. Possibly that was a hindrance there in that small school where a teacher could give so little time to any one pupil. But I am sure he was retained in his grade for other reasons than smartness, for he had plenty "on the ball" when he wanted to apply himself. But he was a cocksure lad, and when final examinations came the spring before for high school, he found himself wanting. He had made his boasts about what he was going to do when his cousin came to teach.

Country School Teacher (1909)

All my fears of a country school were bottled up in me and I trembled for the day that had to come.

On a Saturday afternoon before the opening of school, I was in one of the stores making a purchase.

"Ma, there's the teacher!" I heard a very definite stage whisper not far from where I was standing. There was a little plump girl of about eight standing excitedly near her jolly, round mother who came and spoke to me. They were good friends of my uncle and family and she was very nice to me. But I was all but tongue tied. I had rather hoped I wouldn't have to face the mothers until I started my work.

On the last Sunday before the crack of doom, I went home with my uncle and aunt who always came into our town for church. Only my Creator and I knew how long and earnestly I prayed that night. No new captain ever faced his ranks with more nervousness.

A one room schoolhouse was built in 1881. As attendance grew to over 80 students, this two-story wood building was built in 1886. This is where I taught as a public school teacher in rural Hampton, Nebraska. My first teaching experience, beginning in September 1910. (Courtesy of the Plainsman Museum, Aurora, Nebraska)

Chapter 2
My Tenderfoot Sister (1913)

This original story was written in the mid-1950s. Excerpts were published in the Apple Valley Bonanza weekly newspaper in three installments in January 1966. It tells the story of Erma's sister Ruby and her husband, Dan Hungerford, as they move to the Mojave Desert when Dan gets a new job.

Dan Hungerford and Ruby Patterson were married December 25, 1912, in Nebraska.

I have a sister named Ruby. Everything that is interesting and outrageous happens to her—her life has been more fun than a bucketful of monkeys. In fact, there is a line from Shakespeare's *The Tempest* that fits her to a tee! "I have been in such a pickle since I saw you last." Her first experience at the age of 23 on the Mojave Desert was a riot. Of course, it is a lot funnier when she tells it—but I'll do my best.

Ruby and her husband, Dan Hungerford, were in on the reclamation of the desert in their younger days. He had taken a job reclaiming portions of the Mojave. It was in the later day pioneering years, and things were not as highly mechanized. My sister had been living on the Nebraska prairies. She had been lured to Southern California where they were sure of finding the pot of gold at the end of the rainbow.

It was the land where dreams would come true. Or so they thought. But to their disappointment, there were too many people thinking the same thing. They did not find the pot of gold; nor did they see a vestige of the bow of many colors. So, their dreams had not come true. But they had an experience!

And this is their story. Anyway, it is mostly Ruby's story. But Dan was there in the offing watching over his bride and her response to the desert's challenge. What he missed at the storied end of the rainbow in Southern California he tried to capture in his job as foreman on a large area of homesteads in the middle of the Great Mojave Desert. Neither Dan nor Ruby had ever been on the desert and life there was going to be a new experience in living for the young couple.

The Great Mojave Desert

The time of their hegira into the desert was in the beginning of the 20th century in Fall of 1913. The Great Mojave Desert was just coming into its own and it was now an entity to itself and had long since passed from the stages of fear, hatred and horror for its passersby or residents. Back in the 1880s when the railroads entered California through the desert, thousands of people responded to the railroad companies' efforts to locate people along their rail lines on their own land holdings, which ran into millions of acres.

Agriculture became almost as powerful as the railroads were to satisfy the restless fever of the country that craved new and virgin lands. The building of the railroads and the expansion of farmlands brought into use that great invention of the 'fresno scraper' without which the agriculture, railroad, and construction fields would have advanced less rapidly and would have been less instrumental in doing so much for progress. Additional homestead acts were passed by the government, which benefited the desert areas of the West.

There were many verbal wars between the railroad companies in enticing the people of the nation to enter California. Excursion rates made it possible for the people to travel westward. Family cars were established so that the emigrants could cook their meals and lessen their traveling expenses.

The United States became quite conscious of the desert lands of eastern California. People came west from all sections—the eastern seaboard, the South, the Mid-West. The Gold Rush had brought California into existence. The new country had made itself into a new state. The railroads helped to build up the population. Southern California had overpopulated itself. The result—the desert came into its own.

The people of the United States have always wanted land. The American frontier has changed many times. The desert waited a long time for its day. Jobs had become difficult to find in the southland of California. But Dan was lucky when he drew his foreman job on the desert.

Many homesteaders did not live on their land except for the minimum time required by the government. These people put their property into the hands of agents who looked after the affairs of the absentee homesteaders. The companies contracted to do the land leveling, drilling wells, planting trees, digging ditches, and assuming the duties of proving up on homestead lands for the owners. Many of the homesteaders proved up on their own property and from the ranks of these some very nice ranches developed.

The Mojave River

The reclamation project where the Hungerfords were was about twenty-five to thirty miles from the town of Victorville that had been first settled by a homesteader in 1861. The Victorville settlement was established near the Mojave River where there was a crossing in the early years.

The Mojave River was the lifeline of the desert country and served as a highway for the emigrants coming into the state. The Mojave River has its origin in the San Bernardino Mountains where the headwaters find their way into two main streams which come down the mountains and merge at the foothills. The waters flow against the natural divide and come down on the north and east instead of going as they should toward the Pacific Ocean. The Mojave River proper dips underground when it merges and flows through granite basins for most of its way, passing through a cut in the hills at Victorville and flowing on toward Barstow and to its ultimate end in Afton Canyon, where it flows out onto sand and vanishes. The Mojave River has an ancient heritage which goes back billions of years when it was a river of mighty force.

My reclaimers did not see this odd river when they first came to the desert, for the project was situated west of the town of Victorville. The early roads did not follow the roadways of today. Their home place was five miles from Gray Mountain, which is situated in the Mirage Lake area near today's town of Adelanto and the George Air Base, a government training field for pilots. There is a soaring field there also for gliders. Mirage Lake is one of twelve valleys which comprise what is styled as Victor Valley, the largest of the divisions of the river area, and which has no definite boundary lines.

From Los Angeles to the Desert

Ruby and Dan had been driven from Los Angeles to the desert. The trip had been made at night. My sister cannot explain just why they traveled at night unless time was a factor in getting on the job, or if the weather had something to do with it. They found no macadamized

My Tenderfoot Sister (1913)

roads in those days, and the route was a devious one—winding, rough, sandy, steep and unsure. They had made the trip in a car known to fame and story as a "Tin Lizzie", a product of Ford Motors. They were chauffeured by an agent of the real estate company. My sister slept through the night ride and when she awoke, they were at Lancaster where they stopped for breakfast.

My sister thought that Lancaster was "such a funny little town, set out in the middle of nowhere." She had come straight from the prairie lands of Nebraska to the desert's wide-open spaces. But her former spaces had been fertile ones, and level with green crops of pasturage and orchards and gardens in season. The world that stretched out before her seemed an unlimited one of sand and sage, creosote and Joshua trees.

When they emerged from the eating-house, they saw long-eared jackrabbits hopping over the terrain.

As they rode across the desert, Ruby thought of all she had read of the desert. The hazards and horrors of the early day emigrants. She had sense enough to know that much of all she had read were tales of imagination. But even so, this was a new life for them. The covered wagon era had gone into history, though she was to see many wagons without their hooded tops, for the automobile was not so commonly used just then. Buckboards and buggies and saddle horses were still in frequent use.

A New Home

Gray Mountain, the highest peak of the area, which gave the settlement its name, loomed high and beckoning in the distance, monarch of all it surveyed. It could be the lodestar for their future. Finally, they were at the one-roomed tent house that was to be their home. It was not a very prepossessing picture for the recent bride who had always lived in a spacious house. The sides of the building were made of lumber halfway up its height. Canvas fastened from there to the roof completed the walls. Mosquito netting was tacked over the one window. The door was made of wood.

Gray Mountain near present-day Victorville, CA in the Mojave Desert as it looked in 1913.

A short distance from the house was another tent house a bit longer, which was used as a bunkhouse for the "cowboys" as Ruby called the men who worked for Dan. They were not true cowboys in the sense it was used in the old West.

Dan's work was laid out for him. Ruby unpacked their baggage and prepared meals for them that first day on the Mojave Desert. She stood outside in the falling twilight and looked long and thoughtfully at the horizon lines. An evening breeze came up and the sun went down in a ball of glorious fire, the first of many indescribable sunsets she was to watch, in colors no artist could duplicate. She felt an inward glow as though something beautiful had enfolded her.

She went inside and "set" her bread for the morrow, put her tiny domicile in order, and went to bed, first admonishing Dan to look under the bed for snakes. Tired from the newness of her life, she slept her first night on the Mojave, closing her mind from the things she might like to do or see in this strange land. Her last conscious thought was of the cry of the coyote that came from some distant hill as it sang its requiem of the night. It sounded sad to her.

My Tenderfoot Sister (1913)

All Shining and Bright

It was a rather dreary-looking landscape that stretched out in every direction from where my sister gallantly stood in the middle of the Great Mojave Desert. It was dreary because she had been on that desert for only about twenty-four hours, and she hadn't had a chance to succumb to that legendary threat that the desert's fascination will get you in the course of time!

Dressed in a skirt almost to her ankles, a white starched blouse with long, tapering leg-o'-mutton sleeves, and high-heeled buttoned shoes, Ruby stood tall and straight. She pushed a light tan felt hat back from her forehead and wiped a bit of perspiration from her face. For all that it was the fall of the year, her hike out on a desert had been a warm affair. She wasn't very far from the tent house, but she had walked fast. She gazed to the north, the east, the south, and the west—and she wasn't too sure which direction was which or what. She didn't know where she wanted to go—but go she did want to do. She wasn't sure she was going to like this desert she found herself on, but she sure was going to find out!

She set flashing black eyes on the mystic distances where desert and sky met; she noted the whereabouts of one peak that was higher than the others. That would be Gray Mountain, which towered above a dozen other graduated hills off in the distance. It had a come-on look. It was the goal for the hike she had assigned to herself. She wanted to learn all there was to know about the desert. She had grown up in the Ozark foothills and she knew something about walking and hiking. How she would love to get on a horse again as she had been privileged to do when she was in the Ozarks with her riding club before she had gone with the family to the Nebraska prairies. She hoped things would work out so she could ride one of the ponies she had seen in the corral.

Gray Mountain seemed a very gray looking sight to her that autumn morning. She would hike herself over there and get to the top. Maybe she might find herself a gold mine.

She brushed a tall waving bush that tickled her face as she stooped to look at a low greenish-gray plant growing near the tall bush. Extremes! One hugging close to the ground, the other higher than her head. She grasped at the brownish-green, small-leafed branch that had swept her face and was delighted with the tarry aroma that came from it. She had been given a welcome embrace by a branch of the creosote bush and she liked the smell of it. She hadn't had an opportunity to learn its scientific name, but she rather liked the local names that plants were often given. This bush seemed to be everywhere. She had noticed it from the automobile yesterday and there were some in the area around the tent house. She did not know that she had met up with a typical dry-land plant, but she was to find out that it was the most common of the local desert plants. It was always to be the most delightful desert plant to her.

She had also noted another exceedingly interesting tree, which they called the Joshua. She had seen pictures of it in the real estate office in Los Angeles and they had passed some on the last lap of their trip yesterday morning. There had been a little story tacked to that tree; something about a strange larva that lived in it and that caused the contorted limbs of the shaggy overgrown cactus-appearing plant. Also, the note included the story of it getting its name of Joshua, as it was said to have a scientific name it belonged to the lily family. The emigrating Mormons were said to have given it the name of Joshua as the spreading limbs seemed to be lifting arms in pleas for succor.

But Gray Mountain was her interest for the day—her goal, at least, and she wondered how far away it was. But she had no odometer on her stylish shoes, so she had no idea how far she had already walked or how far the mountain was. But she would make another start and get herself over there.

The sandy soil glittered in the morning's golden sun, and she was entranced with the tumbleweed that took off in the morning wind and tumbled across the desert, flirting with the other loosened plants of its ilk, capering gaily and audaciously nudging one another

My Tenderfoot Sister (1913)

as if in a game. They clutched at and annexed the loose ones, whirling madly off in piled up masses to form great stacks, airy and brown when hemmed in by rocks or other impedimenta such as deadened bushes. The tumbleweeds made her think of children playing a game where they chose sides.

It seemed strange to this girl so recently from the Midwest and who had been used to four seasons that followed a general routine of one season at a time. In the fall, things shouldn't be green, but dead-looking, waiting for winter to cover them with fairy pictures of frost and snow.

Here, there were several colors resplendent in their own shades from late-blooming flowers—or were they weeds?—to so much gray stuff, cheek by jowl with green growing things.

As she plodded over the desert terrain, she let her mind dwell on some of the history she had read of the Mojave Desert. She thought of the tales she had heard of the mines over the desert and dreams of grandeur flashed through her mind. What would it be like to have a mine? To not have to worry about finding jobs and living out on a dreary desert! Surely there must be any numbers of mines in a place like this. What else was it good for? She stepped up her gait and began to take note of where she was so she would not get lost.

In time, she reached her mountain, suddenly realizing she had been thinking seriously about looking for a gold mine. But why shouldn't she? It was usually men that discovered them while they were out looking for a strayed mule or poking around in the rocks with a jack knife. But she had made the mountain—and they had told her it was five miles distant. It hadn't seemed that far! Now she would have to walk back. The mountain was not quite as imposing as she had thought it would be.

Her feet were sore, and her leg muscles ached. The sun had gotten quite warm. It must be about noon. She looked down at her high-top buttoned shoes. They did look pretty silly as a walking shoe and they had grown decidedly uncomfortable. She would have to get herself some high-top elk boots.

Gosh, she was hungry. She started walking around the base of the mountain. Now, wouldn't it be just like her to find gold! Stranger things had happened. She tried to remember stories she had read of the finding of gold. Crevices? Gulches? Stream beds? The small gulches brought no help. She looked under every movable rock she came to. She even pulled bushes away and looked under them in her eagerness. It was as though she was seeking something that was lost.

She climbed upward, slipping back at times, grasping at the low plants and loosening sandy soil. She was totally unconscious of the great vista of the desert that reached to the horizon. She was newly obsessed with the determination to find gold. Neither stark, raw beauty, or the fine points of color and line held her thoughts. She had one thought only—gold.

She thought—if one wants something enough . . . She stopped in her erratic fumbling in the shade of a rock. Merciful heavens! She had found gold. It was there in great quantities, scattered about. It was so beautiful, so shining and glistening, flashing myriads of specks that caught the beams of the sun. It was everywhere. On the hillside, on the floor of the desert where she had slid down in her excitement. She forgot how tired she was. She was no longer hungry. She must get back, though, to tell Dan about her discovery. She was all business. She knew something about mining claims from her reading of the Zane Grey novels. There had to be a stake to make it legal. She found a stick of hard, gray wood from an age-old bush and poked it in the sand. She had no baking powder can in which to leave her name. Neither did she have a pencil or paper to write her notice on. So, she piled rocks around the stake and left it to luck.

"Tenderfoot that I was," she tells us, "I was so excited!" She lifted her long dark skirt and with her strong white teeth tore off a portion of her starched white petticoat and ripped off a long strip, which she tied to the stake, the streamers waving saucily in the desert breeze.

My sister had found her gold without benefit of pick or shovel. In her excitement to get back to the tent house and tell Dan of her luck, she forgot to take samples. There would have to be an assay.

She would take care of that later. She wasn't tired any longer and she took fast, long strides back to the tract and Dan.

Ruby was a convincing person. When she rushed excitedly into the tent house where Dan and the cowboys were having lunch, Dan had the cowboys hitch up the ponies to the buckboard and they all returned with her over her golden trail.

Dan sitting on the buckboard with the cowboys

The sequel was a bit of a come-down. The shining mineral that my sister had discovered was not gold. She was told she had only found mica, or "fool's gold." They had the laugh on her! But she laughed the hardest and longest. She was not the first, nor the last, to make the same mistake.

Ruby is still chuckling over that adventure.

Cactus

After the "fool's gold" misadventure, she said, "Dan let me take the buckboard and I kept on exploring. I would put my dinner in the fireless cooker and start out in the morning at 10 o'clock. By this time, I had gone native and was wearing high-top elk skin boots and divided skirts and I thought I was a real cowgirl!"

She remembers, one of the first things she found was a beautiful cactus in bloom. She dug it up and rushed home and set it out in front of the bunk house. The stickers went clear through her leather gloves, and she tried to pick them out of her fingers with her teeth and got them planted in her tongue. She said, "I felt like a porcupine for a week."

"Dan did not like the idea of a cactus in front of the house, so every time the boys washed, they would throw the soapy water on it trying to kill it. They did not dare dig it up! I practically had to guard it with my rolling pin! Needless to say, it thrived and blossomed in spite of the soap and tobacco spit and became quite a sight for the tourists and land seekers that came. By and by, the real estate men started to bring their prospects by, as I always had something around that was different."

"I went out and gathered wildflowers one day, coming back with over 100 different varieties. I took a picture of them and the real estate agent took the film and had it enlarged and hung in the offices in Los Angeles."

Ruby with her pets including Trixie the St. Bernard laying next to her. Next to Trixie is another dog named Peanut and she is holding a kitty. The box behind Peanut is used to house her reptile pets.

My Tenderfoot Sister (1913)

Desert Pets

"I found a tiny baby jackrabbit once when I opened Dan's dinner bucket. I fed it canned milk and raised it to be a huge buck. The dog and the cat and the jackrabbit were great friends."

"Of course, I had to keep the rabbit penned up for fear he would get the call of the wild and run off. One day when I was in Los Angeles, 'Jackie' came up missing. I also found out another person on the project had rabbit stew that day."

"A blue-bellied horned toad jumped out of the dinner bucket one day. He was the cutest pet of all the ones I had during my sojourn on the desert. He would go with me on my 'exploring' trips. I tied a string to his leg and put him in my shirt pocket. I fastened the other end of the string to a buttonhole. He would crawl out on my shoulder and look me in the eye so cunningly. I had to turn Blue Belly loose when I went to Los Angeles as the "boss's" wife said she would not look after my menagerie, and I was afraid he or she—I never knew the sex—would not like the city traffic and my friends might not like him."

"Seeing my cat's fur standing on end out in the yard, I investigated and found him spitting and spatting at a big dry land turtle. So, I had another pet. I tied him up and made a marvelous pet of him. My neighbors cooked all the turtles they found as they were considered very fine eating. I never could bring myself to eat Pokey. They told me after I left the desert that Pokey stayed around the house for a long time."

"There being no gas on the desert then, my reclaimers had an old-fashioned kitchen wood stove to cook on. They burned what they called petrified wood, which was only decayed yucca trees, full of holes, but which made a grand fire." One day Ruby tossed some wood in the stove from the wood box that had been filled by one of the boys and started a fire. There, crawling out from under a piece of wood was a "darling lizard" which she rescued from cremation.

She tied up her latest menagerie specimen and attempted to make a pet of it, but she didn't like its hard, "sarcastic" look after Blue Belly's gentleness, so turned it loose.

Her next pet was a beautiful diamond back rattler—pet for the length of time it took to admire its back! With her quaint way of understanding reptile and animal characteristics, she disliked the defiant look on sight.

The coyotes were obnoxious, particularly as they ate up the harness and every bit of leather they could get to. The coyotes howled and the panthers screamed for the city-bred girl. At first it wasn't so good, but later it became music to her ears, and she began to listen for the evening songs of the wild. She was doing pretty good in her efforts to go western.

Master Painter

The desert had gotten her. She loved the gloriously beautiful sunsets. She would sit on the wood pile every evening and wish to be a master painter. The air was exhilarating. When she had to go into the city, she felt suffocated and couldn't get back to the wide-open spaces fast enough.

Like all cowgirls, she had the urge to ride, that sister of mine. She had been a good rider in the Ozark Hills where we had been raised and nothing daunted her in such matters. She recalled, "There was an old fellow that had a claim nearby that had the most beautiful horse. He was a big, beautiful, pacing stallion. I rode him to the country store. He saw some other horses there and I had a sweet time getting him home. I rode in like Napoleon who had conquered the world and sighed for more worlds to conquer. My world tumbled down when Dan told me I could not ride that horse anymore. He got me a saddle and let me ride Dick—one of the ponies I had been driving the buckboard." After that she was content to ride one of her ponies.

Her ponies were never separated, except when she rode horseback, and then they would cry for one another. She usually rode the one named Dick. One time, Dick, in his grief at being away from Brownie, paid no attention to where he was going and stepped into a squirrel hole and they both went down. Dick always took her safely home if she wandered too far afield on the confusing desert trails.

Ruby with her ponies, Dick and Brownie.

Between her walking over desert ground looking for lovely flowers that spread out a carpet for Spring for her, her horse-back riding, and the buckboard that she shared with her dog and gun, she managed to see a lot of the desert in those early days when distances were far between settlements and between homesteads.

But it gave her a chance to store up in her subconscious many beauties of her lonely, quiet, but satisfying world that has never left her and now appear on some beautiful oil paintings that she loves to create. Her love and understanding of grouping colors that are natural has never left her. Be it a faraway horizon, a blazing sunset, a moon over a desert waterhole—there are mirages impressed upon her subconscious and in her understanding of desert reliefs and stark, raw beauty.

Ruby with Dan's cow, Bossy. Gray Mountain is in the background.

They had an old cow that Dan milked. At least she had him. This was quite an addition to their pioneer pastoral scene. Dan was the apple of her cow-eye. She followed him wherever he worked, even if it was ten miles away. They put a bell on her so they could always find her—not that there was any worry about Bossy not keeping up with her master. My sister began to depend on hearing the cowbell to have their evening dinner ready.

On rainy days, the cow would stand at the door and wait for Dan to go out to his chores and would follow him back like a huge dog. Once, while waiting for him, she grew so anxious she proceeded to go into the house, managing to get her head and front feet inside. It took some coaxing along with pulling and pushing to get her to back out. Ruby was glad it was Dan the cow adored; otherwise, she would have had many difficult times when she was there alone with Bossy.

Trips to Victorville

They bought their groceries in Victorville. She often made the trip alone. It took her about four hours to make the trip which was 35 miles by unworked dirt roads. She carried her revolver with her, placed on one side of the buckboard seat, her St. Bernard dog, Trixie, on the other, as she was deputized to carry the mail.

"I had to protect Uncle Sam!" she laughs now as she retells the experiences of those colonizing days.

She beat the monotony of the trip by conversing with her dog and shooting at snakes. "I really got a thrill out of it," she says. "But I never could look the reptiles in the face. I had always heard that if one did that it would be fatal. I would, or might, succumb to their charms!" She scoffs, "I was afraid, particularly of the sidewinders who give no warning, but strike from either side."

"Once I went to Victorville for 200 fruit trees to be set out," she recalls. "I had to stay all night. I put my horses in a corral behind a grocery store. I managed to get the harness off the ponies, Brownie and Dick."

My Tenderfoot Sister (1913)

Ready for a trip to Victorville, Ruby with Dick and Brownie.

"I thought I was quite western! But the next morning when I went out to hook up, I got the part that goes over the tail over the ears and had such a terrible time that a fellow whom I took to be a city guy came over and asked if I needed help. I had to admit, all my western conceits gone, that I did. He hooked it up for me and took the team to the town water trough and went with me for the nursery stock."

"The nurseryman thought he was my hired man (dressed up!) and handed him a spade and put him to work digging trees. He went at it nonchalantly, and later refused pay for his work. I never knew who he was, but he was probably some new settler, too."

The Kingdom of the Sun

They came into the valley that had been silent for so long. Came and left the best of what they had, giving not only the physical hardness and courage, but the culture they had acquired elsewhere. It was all a part of the building of the little empire in the Kingdom of the Sun. Pioneers, you are saluted; you who have helped to carve a mighty West.

I have taken "Kingdom of the Sun" for the title for this section because it so well clarifies how the people felt who came there hoping to stay. It is the title of a social magazine brought out by the people of the valley, brought out in 1913 and 1914 and printed on light buff-colored heavy paper. The magazine, copies of which one of the instigators, Raymond "Penny" V. Morrow of Oro Grande, placed at my disposal, was twelve inches long by six inches wide. In the few copies printed and distributed (several times a year) is a very complete story of the life of the residents in Victor Valley. They were published by Lillian D. Gregory N.D. of Oro Grande, CA. As stated on the rear wrapper, it was "Filled with the Lure of the Desert, and the Charm of the Vast Mojave" and was "For Women, By Women, To Women."

My sister tells of a dry lake a short distance from their acreage. It is about five miles wide and 10 miles long, as she remembers. The mirages that settled over the lake were beautiful—though confusing. She saw great cities, castles, meadows, and once a large water lake with a ship at anchor. She tells, now, laughingly, that at Christmas time she was sure she saw Santa Claus with his sleigh and reindeer!

And the weather—they had all kinds, as the desert never fails to produce. The sandstorms which were frequent and disagreeable; the small whirlwinds of powdered sand and leaves—of shrubs; and when it rained, it poured!

All sorts of people came into the colony to take up desert claims. Among them was a famous opera singer. As he rode his horse home, day or evening, early or late, from wherever he may have been, he sang. Faintly, from the distance they would hear him, and it was soothing. As he drew nearer the tents and bunkhouses at night, the singing was so beautiful they would sit up in bed and listen until it completely died away. The singer had come there from New York. He was very eccentric. One time he walked almost all the way home from Victorville because he thought his horse was tired.

She tells of the lone woman homesteader who kept small stacks of wood near her doorstep and inside the crude cabin, handy to use on the fearsome snakes that came too near for comfort.

My Tenderfoot Sister (1913)

The settlers included educators, lawyers, doctors, and farmers; those who were experienced and in the making; old and young; people just starting out in life on their own; people remaking their lives; those who loved the great outdoors of the desert and those who hated it. Many stayed close to the settlements on Mojave's tricky banks; others were more content to settle on the lonelier places. There were people whose pasts could not bear investigation, but mostly they were people whose lives were open books.

The Kingdom of the Sun waits under changing conditions. Waits for the modern way of progress. But it is not so sleepy. Highways lead past old ranches, some of them abandoned, some used for cattle ranges. Others have grown into desert towns.

The yucca trees and the great spread of wildflowers deck the desert in Spring. Trails led back into mines and the rockhounds and the geologists explore out of the way places for hidden interests. The skies are still so blue.

The coyotes are less plentiful than when they sang of the wild to my sister, but even yet, they run along the lonelier highways or along the riverbanks and copses. The old trails are there, many obliterated by homes and towns, but if you listen you will hear the great silences that my sister knew.

Chapter 3
Lone Tree School (1919)

Written in the mid-1950s. Erma moves from Madera, CA to Fallon, NV to be the first teacher of a pioneer one-room schoolhouse.

Teaching in Berenda, from September 1918 to December 1918 when I was forced to rest after a bout of the Spanish Flu.

It was in the middle of March 1919 that I left my home in Madera, California to cross the state line to take a position in a small, delightful valley in Nevada, as teacher of the Lone Tree school. The phrase 'The Ides of March' flashed through my brain when I thought of the date that morning as I left Reno to go down into the valley. I little realized then just why the prophetic phrase might be symbolic for me. It was a beautiful trip down. Uphill and downhill, past lovely, wooded country, gliding by tree-lined rivers that rushed through that uneven county. I had made an acquaintance on the train that had told me a good deal of the country into which I was going. He had been a friend of Peter B. Kyne's, and I was all agog with interest in his stories.

I had been without a position for several months following a severe case of the Spanish Flu and for that reason was starting a school in the middle of the spring term. It seemed that this was a new school district I was going to. I was to be the first teacher in the newly organized school. I pictured it all so very spick and span and new. The enchantment of the unknown was upon me. Romance played hide and seek with all sorts of daydreams in my excited brain. This going into new places always held glamour for me. My boarding place had been arranged for me. I knew nothing about that except for the name of the people I was to stay with.

Fallon Railroad Station (Courtesy of the Churchill County Museum, Fallon, Nevada)

Lone Tree School (1919)

Fallon, Nevada

The School Superintendent met me at the little railroad station. He was a very handsome, big, splendid man. My heart turned over with several pity-pats. But he was very business-like. He fairly threw me in the car and took me to his office in the courthouse where I sat and sat. We weren't having sit down strikes in the school business, but I sat anyhow. It seemed my prospective landlady, some six or eight miles out in the country was having trouble with her car and could not get in to meet me. (Cars do have sit down strikes.) There was nothing for me to do but to sit. My handsome Romeo was a very busy man and paid very little attention to me. (I found out afterward, months afterwards, that he was very bashful.) And that he was single, too. Well, he was to have enough of me later, so it was just as well that he did not fall for my particular style of charm. He had to take me to lunch—for he was a gentleman.

Fallon Courthouse is on the right. To the left is the Churchill County Jail. (Courtesy of the Churchill County Museum, Fallon, Nevada)

My sit-down strike continued in that dusty little office that he shared with an attorney, until late in the afternoon when a personage called for me. A striking woman, just reaching forty. Fair, fat and forty, filled the bill. Something clicked immediately. She awed me. I was little, and slim, and dark—sort of forlorn from a night's travel and a day's sit down strike. She laughed. A merry, ringing, trickling laugh. It went into me—struck a cord and we were in tune. I thought—how lucky I was. But, to my disappointment, she was not to be my landlady. She was a neighbor living a few miles farther out from where I was to teach and live. It seemed my landlady's car was still on a strike and she had telephoned this Mrs. C. to ask her to get me and bring me out. So, I was again loaded into a Ford—me and my baggage—with a whole seat full of books that were to be delivered to the schoolhouse.

We started country ward. Out toward the mountains. Past the sage brush. Evening was about to fall. Mountains, towering to the front of me. To the left, to the right. Charge of the bright brigade—Blue, brown, gold. High and low. They penned us in. But they are forever beautiful in my memory—those mountains out there where the shadows fell. Houses, not too close together. Not too far apart. Past barbed wire fences. Cattle, goats. Irrigation ditches. Finally, the house. Little, and low—but not so old. Set off alone in a big expanse of ground. Unpainted. Two windows to the front. In the dim evening light, I saw a tack of hay and a corral. It had the lonely look of a homestead. A light shined through a window. I was ushered into the little house. Three rooms, one right after the other. A man and a woman and a little child. A tiny girl of seven. I wondered where I was to sleep. A kitchen, a dining room and one bedroom. But I was tired, and I was hungry. Sit downers do get hungry. True western hospitality awaited me. My landlady, blue-eyed and auburn-haired and lovely and interesting. Her husband—typically western. You could not call anyone with a heart of gold uncouth. The little girl—just one to love; a steaming supper waiting for me.

Lone Tree School (1919)

Goodbye, Mrs. C. We have met and I am yours. I came, I saw, and we both conquered. We were destined to be friends. Thank God, we can choose our friends. You know where I am. Come back. I feel lost in this big, wide, beautiful country. But I await the dawn of the first school day.

The following day, Mrs. F. took me to the clerk of the school board. A strange woman. Another couple with just one child. They were people that lived completely to themselves. The advent of the new school in the district was the means of bringing people together. Of finding out about their characters and dispositions. I went to sign my contract. I was temporarily being certified until the spring examinations were given as the state in which I held certification was not honored in this state. I signed. Some very few moments afterwards Mrs. Clerk asked me if I would take a special examination if the Superintendent would give it to me. I declined. Haughtily.

"And, why?"

"I have my certificate. It has been accepted by the state of Nevada. It is not necessary for me to go through that. I came to teach." I must have set my little square jaw. I had the bull by the horns. My contract was signed.

She had a jaw too. And it set. And it stayed set. Talk about sit down strikes. She was the woman who had seldom been in another woman's home in more than ten years. Her child had never been to any school. She had been taught at home. She was a lovely child, though. She had isolated herself for all these years, but at the coming of this new school, she had been selected as one of the fitting women for the job of conducting the business affairs of the school.

I had been in the workforce for years and I felt I knew a little bit about what I should do and should not do. So, I refused to take an unnecessary examination, and she never forgave me for balking. The Ides of March. I met them when I refused to do her first bidding.

Fairview mining town. In the foreground is a prospector. The schoolhouse in the back center would be moved in 1919 to Fallon to be the first Lone Pine Schoolhouse. (Courtesy of the Churchill County Museum, Fallon, Nevada)

My New School

School opened. All the mothers in the district were there. I began to think I was to teach both mothers and children. And before the terms ended, I knew I should have had some of the mothers in my school as pupils. I had to ask them to leave in order to get the children down to business and open up my work.

The schoolhouse was not new. It had been hauled down, with all the equipment from a piano to a water bucket and tin cup, from an abandoned mountain mining camp (Fairview Mining Camp). There were the battle scars of other years on the woodwork. The stove in the middle of the floor. The teacher's desk on the little raised platform at what was the front of the room, but which was really the back of the room. I faced the front—and only door. The pupils faced me. All but one. The little lone chick of Mrs. Clerk. Her mother wanted her seat turned to face the door so she could see her home when the door was open and she looked out. I allowed it. I relaxed my jaw on that score. I did feel sorry for that dear little kid. She did not know how to mingle or to play or to meet others.

I do not know when it first began. I was so interested. I had come over to teach. I did teach. I loved every moment of it. The weather was beautiful. I could look out on trees that lined the irrigation ditches nearby. The sky was always blue. An ardent, luring, beautiful blue. And there were always my mountains—off there where the shadows fell. Pheasants lurked out in the school yard. The cry of the pheasant in the copse is so strange and so beautiful. We loved it—those little folks and me. We always raised our heads a bit and listened intently when we heard the cry of the pheasant. Like all beautiful things, it came seldom, and we waited for it—and enjoyed it. The piano was so grand to have. I was so glad now that my mother had used her own special brand of insistence in days gone by about my music lessons. I could play for these little folks—not to say anything about the pleasure it gave me to have the instrument and get my own release from the ivory keys.

There was the little girl who rode with me every day in the old buggy behind the temperamental horse. She was a thing to love. The little girl. There was the little one somewhat older who sat with her face to the front—or to the back that was really the front. There was a little boy, too, who was an only child. He was destined to be on "the other side," too. There was the little girl from just outside the district, but who came to me because my school was the closest. There was the littler girl than she who was a little orphan, and who lived at her home. She had been raised up to that year in the orphan's home. She was a sad little mixture. She seemed starved for love. I gave it to her. But she paid me back in funny coin. She was a bit mischievous, but I pitied her and when I had to discipline her, I tried to do it gently. I had her lay her little head down on her arms on her desk. That was my method of punishment. But it was like—was it Medusa's head? It doubled and doubled in proportion when it was told until it got about that I was being quite severe—hitting with tin-edged rulers, and such other awful stuff. (There was never a ruler of any sort in the room.)

There was a brother and sister who were just finishing the eighth grade. Nice kids. They came to school on horseback. There was the little Shane girl [reference to 1953 movie Shane.] She was about 12 years old. She worshiped me. She had no father. He was dead. They were a lovely family but poor and struggling.

I loved Mary. She was such a little old woman. She used to stay after school and help me with the cleaning. We always had the little schoolhouse looking so clean and smelling sweet. That sweet, musty smell, that goes in houses of learning, whether little and drab and out of the way—or big and polished and grand and on a city campus.

United States Flag in 1919. Forty-eight stars, before Alaska and Hawaii entered the union.

Lone Tree School (1919)

The Flag

There was often a tug at the heart as we took the flag down and closed the door behind us. One night I forgot to take the flag down. I didn't think of it until about nine o'clock at night when my landlord was asleep and my landlady baking bread. I never smelled homemade bread—if such a miraculous thing ever happened—but I think of the dreadful feeling of guilt and the awful tingling that went up my spine when I came to that evening and had no conscious thought of having taken the flag down. I will feel just that way if I am ever convicted of doing wrong. It was like a nightmare. It must have been pictured on my face. (My face must have been terribly blank for a picture to show. It is a blank page that writing or drawing shows upon, or a blank record that takes an impression of sound.)

"What on earth is the matter? Are you sick? You look awful!"

I felt my hair standing straight up. I had a vague rumor somewhere that it was an offense—actually a crime to leave a flag out at night.

"Oh, I think—I know, I forgot to take the flag down! Oh, what will I do? What will happen to me?"

"For heaven's sake! Do you suppose they—do you suppose anyone has seen it? Come on, I'll take the bread out of the oven, and I will drive you over. Be quiet. Let's don't wake the others."

But the car was on a sit down strike again. It would not budge. It was in league with the enemy. We worried and giggled, to hide our worry. Worried some more. Made all sorts of noise. Two criminals. Rather, a criminal and an accessory. We started to hitch up old dobbin to the shay when the husband came out to see what we were trying to do at that ungodly hour.

"My gosh! Do you suppose they saw it?" They—we were all afraid of they. More about them. He settled the strike and the old car went.

"Don't turn on any lights. Keep as quiet as you can and get that flag down." We all felt guilty. I can still feel that tightening of my heart at my oversight. To myself I was a criminal. I had been disloyal to my flag. That flag that was my duty to teach honor about. I had done something that might get me "in Dutch" with the government.

Two guilty conspirators. We got the old glory down and tossed it into the schoolhouse. Backed out and went home. I fully expected to be arrested the next day.

Troubles

There were three other little folks. Two little boys and one little girl. They lived closest to be school. Their parents were foreigners. Hearts as big as mountains. The mother, big and auburn haired. She wasn't so foreign, and they had a very American name. The father was very dark and talked a bit of broken English. They stood by me staunch and strong.

There was some sort of grape vine system out there in that little country district. The first thing we just knew it. They were having a terribly hard time trying to get everyone else to say something about me so they could fire me. This Mrs. Clerk had never gotten over the fact that I had set my jaw that day when she asked me to take an examination. She had taken her child out of school the next week.

She sowed seeds of discontent in the minds of the lady with the one little boy. Then came the third woman—the one with the one child and the little orphan. They formed a triumvirate to haul my little empire down. The battle was on. War was waged for all we were worth. Everywhere I went I heard how they had tried to get something on me so they could discharge me. Like a battered general, I held the fort. The handsome Romeo of my first day came to school. He had me put the pupils through their classes. This did me credit. I was up on my toes, of course, but I was doing it as my daily chore. He left, giving me some advice about the law of that state allowing us to spank only on the place that nature provided. I thought that was the funniest thing for a Superintendent to say to a teacher—especially when I had no mean pupils and had never had to punish. The last straw came when I went out to take the census and found that two of the triumvirate had proceeded me at every house and was making

Lone Tree School (1919)

a last effort to get a petition to fire me. I went home boiling mad. On top of that, Mrs. Clerk had telephoned my landlady asking if her little girl liked me and if I was good to her.

"One cannot live in the same house with anyone for several weeks and not know her."

Words were spoken from the other end of the line.

"I ought to be able to size up anyone that lives with me. Well, wait a minute. I'll ask the kid. Sister, has the teacher ever whipped you?"

"Whipped me?" A gleam of mischief in the blue eyes of the little fairy that sat on my lap. "Of course not."

"How absurd! Of course she didn't. Well, you can believe anything you want to, but I would have seen anything like that. They have the best time in the world. We are fond of her. She couldn't hurt a fly."

Click.

"Well, I'll be darned." The honest anger of a friendly man.

"It's been going on behind your back for some time. I have hated to tell you. But that day the Superintendent was at school, he was at her house for one hour for lunch. She phoned to see if she could borrow butter. She wanted me to know she was having him at her house."

A heartache. I had been successful at other places in other years. I had somehow made a mistake here in the little district among the people I loved.

"I feel like going home. I am going to write a letter to the Superintendent and tell him my side of it."

I did. A masterpiece of anger and justice.

Exhibit – Teaching Experience

```
FOLLOWING IS RECORD BEFORE MARRIAGE WHEN I WAS ERMA PATTERSON:
Teaching experience:

1910-1911   Rural - 8 Grades      Hampton, Nebraska,        9 Months
      (July 1911 to Sept. 1913 in office of Recorder of
       Deeds, Hamilton County, Nebraska.)

1913-1914   Intermediate grades, Center, Colorado           9 Months

1914-1915   Intermediate grades  Marquette, Nebraska        9 Months

1915-1916   Rural - 8 grades and  1st year of High
                       School---   Meeteetse, Wyoming       6 Months

1916-       Village - 8 grades    Sargents, Colorado        7 Months.

      (January 1917 to Sept 1917  office work in California)

1917-1918   Intermediate grades  Marquette, Nebraska        9 Months

1918-       Rural - 8 grades      Berenda, California       4 Months
                      (Special permit)

1919-       Rural  8 Grades       Fallon, Nevada            3 Months
              (Pioneered this school during its first
               term of only three months)

1919-1920   4th grade and Playground Supervisor
                                   Fallon, Nevada          10 Months

          (June 1920 to June 1921 office of San Joaquin
           Light and Power Corporation - Madera, Calif. )

1921-1922   6th grade  C          Carson City, Nevada      10 Months

                                         Total         76 Months
```

At Lone Pine School, Erma joined as a "temporary certified teacher" from March 1919 to June 1919, a three-month term near Fallon, Nevada. Erma would be the first teacher as a pioneer of Lone Tree School. She was brought on officially the following school year as a certified teacher, Sept. 1919 to June 1920, as a fourth grade teacher and Playground Supervisor.

Chapter 4
Bide A Wee Ranch (1922)

Written in 1935 (while living in Riverside, CA). After Erma and Wilfred (Bill the Engineer) Peirson married on September 3, 1922, in Walnut Creek, CA, they followed a dream and started a family. Bide A Wee is a ranch they owned outside of Madera and lost due to financial circumstances.

Wilfred R. Peirson married Erma Mae Patterson, September 3, 1922, in Madera, CA.

The pioneer blood that ran in both Bill's veins and mine cropped out about three months after we were married. To the ghosts of our ancestors, it probably looked rather tame, but before we were through with our efforts of establishing Bide A Wee Ranch, we had experienced all the financial ups-and-downs, the worries and heartaches attending beloved soil and the dread of the crumbling of our bright air castles, which while not in Spain, were just as thrilling and satisfying.

As do most couples who marry, we wanted a home of our own, to have children, and put foundations under us for the sunset years of our life. I had continued on with my job as billing clerk at a lumber mill to help hurry the fulfillment of those dreams of conquest and peace. It was 1922, and salaries not being what they had once been, it seemed the sensible thing to do at the moment.

Twenty Acres

By methods of inquiry and enthusiasm, Bill stumbled onto an unimproved twenty-acre tract, five miles from the Madera County seat where we both held positions. We had saved enough money finally to which we figured would build us our little castle, the pioneer urge within us not demanding anything palatial. Here was a chance to provide (sweet dreams!) for our future with a bit of good old Mother Earth beneath our feet, a roof above our heads, at least four walls around us. The space thrown in would provide for gardening, chickens, fruit trees, stock and a dog or two for good measure.

This all seemed to mean a certain amount of security for us and our unborn children. Now, whether this air castle would emerge as a sort of homestead or a show place did not at the time matter. The fact that did matter was that it would be a haven of love and security for those little people of our dreams, and a place for us to spend our old age in! All we knew about Ham and Eggs then was the ham we bought at our pet meat market—and hoped someday to raise!—and our chickens were to lay the eggs! And while I knew a girl who knew

Bide A Wee Ranch (1922)

the man, we had yet to learn of the Townsend Plan! [Later to be known as Social Security.]

So, we contracted for our little California ranch, having bought it from a private party, who sort of caught the enthusiasm we had, and wrote the contract to read like a fairy tale. There was nothing to pay down, and not even interest for a couple of years. That to start with and about four hundred dollars in the bank! We were plutocrats and landed gentry! We were young and full of enthusiasm. We both had employment that would keep the wolf from the door, pay the insurance premium that protected the fairy godfather, take care of the water rights—and we found a thousand and one other matters. But we had the world by the tail with a downhill hold—we thought!

I have often wished since that I could have peered into Bill's mind as he walked over those un-ploughed acres and have discerned minutely what he was thinking. Perhaps I might understand more clearly the visions that floated before his land-hungry eyes. Then I could see only the bare ground and the big, empty redwood barn. The plot we had bought had once been a part of a large grain ranch that fell to the sub-dividing stage in a big land boom. The massive, pigeon-infested barn fell to our tract.

I wasn't one to spoil a dream, and as to the right of me, to the left of me, in front of and behind me I saw illustrations of what water and work and visioning could do to barren spaces, I went in for the fairy tale head over heels.

If anyone thinks a twenty-acre California ranch grows beautiful right out of a Chamber of Commerce bulletin, he has a few years of disappointment, discouragement and heartaches along with the thrills. But we had our barn to start with—and the most beautiful western view in this land of natural masterpieces. I look back in memory and wonder how we survived the great ache of beauty that was all around us. It was gorgeous at sundown, and on the moonlighted nights the beauty was ethereal. There were no waterfalls to jump into when the ache became too great, and there were no high precipices to jump from when the too heavenly moon got past bearing. There is too much saneness in a broad California valley to encourage one to end the tortured ache in a mere irrigation ditch—and so we didn't burst with the beauty—we just stored it up for memories.

Little Castle

I immediately took advantage of the fact that I was working for a lumber concern and could get building materials at cost. We got an estimate of what it would take to build a house. Bill drew plans for a compact, convenient little dwelling of three rooms and bath plus that boon of a screened-in back porch. We secured the services of an elderly carpenter, a friend of the family who had no interest toward jerry-building. It took all the money we had saved, more than the same amount that our credit was good for at a bank, and a moral mortgage on our salaries to put up the little California box house and to start improving the soil.

Within two months after we became landowners, we moved into our domicile. It did something to our souls to know it was ours. The floor beneath us was paid for even if the soil beneath that was yet to be freed from debt. I have lived in better houses—and hope to live in still better ones—but there will never be any house so rapturously beautiful, so serene and comforting this side of paradise as was that little ranch house that never got beyond the boarded walls outside, nor the gray building paper that finished the inside. Built of the cheapest of lumber, standing dwarfed and unpainted in the shadow of the massive redwood barn, it was a thing of beauty to us then—and a joy forever in our memories. It was a haven of rest for us at the close of exacting office days.

Bill did the painting on the woodwork while I cooked our meals on the kerosene stove or sat hemming rose colored curtains for the casement windows. In time we wired it for electric lights, although we started with the old "coal oil" lamps, graduating first to the Coleman gasoline lamp and lantern, thence to electricity.

Bide A Wee Ranch (1922)

Bill assembled our first radio. We moved it to our bedside at night and took turns with the earphones. We moved the dinner table beside it so that we wouldn't miss a thing!

We bought a share in the community telephone company. It didn't matter that a couple of years later, when our first baby was about to be born, and we needed the telephone in the dead of the night that it wouldn't work! We possessed one even though it was almost as antiquated as the ones our fathers boasted of forty years before.

Of course, we had to have a car, and that was no small item financially. We went to work each morning before nine o'clock and came home every day right after five to enjoy the sunset and feed the chickens and the white turkeys—and play with the rollicking Airedale. Bill's work with the County Agent took him out many nights and I always went along. But we always went HOME first! There was something so satisfying about jumping into that battered and weathered ranch-commuting car, picking up a few groceries and driving into the setting sun.

From time to time, we added comfortable furniture—when there was any money left over to spare after paying the water bills, the insurance premium, putting in the sceptic tank, the electric pumping plant, paying for the services of a ranch hand, planting fig and apricot trees. The water rights were a heavy burden. They had to be paid whether or not the water was used. The baby fig and apricot trees needed frequent irrigation. Most often this had to be done by moonlight—or if in the dark of the moon the water came to our turn, by the light of the Coleman lantern.

The little trees had to be whitewashed and cultivated. But it was all fun. Fun to sit on the banks of the ditches and watch Bill turn the water this way and that way and listen to the tree frogs and the katydids. It was fun to wield the brush on a Saturday afternoon and smear whitewash on the little trees and vision the day when they would repay us with the milky white of the figs and the golden glow of the apricots.

Feeding the chickens at our Madera ranch.

Although we spent every cent we made on the ranch, pinching and scrimping on our clothes and food and car, we were in the class of millionaires at sunset time with our beautiful view and later when the moonlight lay over our little abode, a cascade of silver lifted it from the obscure little box-like affair into a shining small mansion.

We barely had our lumber bill paid (thank goodness!) when I found my work at the mill was ended. A former employee had returned to town, needed the work, and as I never had any doubt that she was more proficient at billing than I, I never blamed them for re-instating her and letting me out. But it played havoc at the time.

Bide A Wee Ranch (1922)

Job Changes

I was not long out of a job, however, finding temporary work with the Chamber of Commerce, where I had all the gorgeous looking ranches to look at on their advertising that any ranch mad person could dream over to the heart's content! Contacts here led to a place as a reporter on one of the dailies of our town. That meant long hours on foot as I could not afford a car for myself, and the town wasn't large enough for street cars. I certainly kept my girlish figure that year! They used to say I covered the ground about as quickly on foot as some people would have in a car, considering parking problems, traffic, and everything! This was a morning paper, and I had to work fast and furious to be through by five o'clock to ride home with Bill and feed my soul on the beauties of the countryside and the never-failing picture in the western sky.

After six months of reporting, I jeopardized my job by going on several weeks' vacation, so when I returned there was another siege of looking for work. But the same God that looks after fools and kids looks after working wives who try to aid a man to keep a home afloat, and so I found a job in a hardware store.

This gave us another break. We were needing plows and other paraphernalia for cultivating the little trees that for the most part were making a big effort to outwit the alkali that was popping up its ugly head. Again, I was able to supply, at cost, a great need.

When summer vacation time rolled around, the boss' daughters were home from school—and so the hardware job was handed over to them. But the fine hand of economics had been working like a shuttle in a loom. The lumber mill had been the means of getting our building done at a minimum cost, not to speak of the fire fuel that came from the same place. The Chamber of Commerce gave me contacts—and whetted my ranch-mad soul, and the newspaper brought me countless friends and a great interest in humanity. The hardware store provided, at cost, the farming implements. I mustn't neglect to state that all this time friend husband remained in the position where he was getting expert information and advice from the best authorities in the nation on how to run our ranch.

I had one last whirl at urging the ranch to a future when I went into a county position, working under the horticultural commissioner. I was submerged, by this time, along with Bill in the emphatic need of saving what we had already invested. We had to somehow save the little ranch until the time it would give us returns for our worried, tender care, and the enthusiasm that still was with us, though it had reached a heart-breaking stage. The ranch had to be nourished, even as a child does in its tenderest years. We lived a good deal on hopes in those days, but we held to the light that someday the property would enhance in value and pay us well for the dreaming of our dreams.

Our first born, James Marlow Peirson, September 5, 1925.

Bide A Wee Ranch (1922)

A New Addition

The stork ended the county job. We had always looked forward to the time when we could afford a baby. But to working people that time never seems to come, so God himself has to take a hand. But we were truly happy, because we didn't get younger with the years, and hadn't we made this brave effort to establish a home for just such occasions?

Half the salary was gone. But that wasn't all. The trees began to give up the ghost and die. The soil, with the advent of water upon it, began to turn slowly to alkali. Bills piled up. Bill's job received a cut in pay until it hardly afforded our food and clothes and transportation, let alone nourish the ranch. And now we had other responsibilities—greater far than any other.

It was a beautiful experience, having my first baby. Nature had been good to me. I was fundamentally healthy, and the gods were kind to my looks and form and I was able to stay on at the office longer than was the usual thing. I often wondered what the ghosts of my maternal ancestors thought of me. But hadn't they put their hand to the plough—and looked neither forward or backward? I was living in a modern time—and I was playing the game—to help. We were pioneering under different circumstances. The war of our generation had passed, and we had a different outlook on life—but we were essentially made of the same stuff.

It had been a satisfying experience to help my husband financially as well as to mend his socks and cook his meals, but now I had the biggest job on earth!

My little first-born son! My precious baby! A war was behind me. How could I think then that he came along just in time to grow up to bring me the fears and worries Bill's mother had had in 1917. [A son going to war.]

End of a Dream

I often wonder why it is that when the babies begin to come that finances run. Of course, our babies had nothing to do with that in our family. It was simply that depression had caught up with us. The clean-cut surgery of Bill's appropriation ended the dream and we became submerged completely with the ranch.

Little James in the front yard.

For it is gone—the little ranch we had named Bide A Wee—and where we bided, a while. Somehow we have lived through it. But a strong man's heart broke. The vision became blurred. The trees didn't return our care and love with the white or the golden fruit. In fact, the treason soil we had run so blithely over in those first months and years had turned traitor to us and spoilt our dreams.

The little doll house we built with so many dreams and so much labor of love has burned to the ground. I hate fire, but somehow if we could not go on living in it, the news that reached us months after we had gone away did not hurt so much. No one else's dreams went into the building of that low, boxed affair. No other's hopes were painted into the gray woodwork. No other man's labor of love had put in the septic tank that his family might have the modern convenience of a bathroom while pioneering virgin soil. It was his pick and shovel that had turned the hurrying waters around the little trees that tried so hard to "make a go of it." It was his hands that laid the wires for the electricity that brightened our little corners, and his ingenuity that assembled the radio that we might keep a pace with the world's events. It was no other couple's sweet baby whose breath became entangled in the soft, gray tones of the building paper on the enfolding walls.

When all the labor of our hands and hearts went into nothing, it was just as well for it to be buried there in the soil where I had tried to raise grass and flowers, and where only the sturdy marigold pushed its shining face out of the treasoned soil we had once loved and tried so hard to build a home upon. It is all there—our dreams, with the golden and crimson sunsets we never tired of, a daily pyre for the burial.

New ventures have come, and always new visions rise to replace the old. But he works alone now as far as the earning power is concerned. Though I still "work", it is confined to the routine of homebuilding. Ironing little print dresses, creating a couple of dozen Shirley Temple curls on the head of the little princess who queens it over a fond daddy is work. And so is washing, ironing and mending pairs and pairs of little socks and countless shirts and cords and overalls for a couple of rowdy little boys!

There is food to think about to build sturdy little bodies, and ways and means to plan for the little extra things that children have a right to expect. There is always the fun of making friends, working with the teachers, helping to keep a P.T.A. alive, and always that great and glorious job of helping a good man to keep his dreams.

Ah, not one iota of it all would I exchange for the swankiest of sables in the downtown windows. A battered piano, a pair of tap shoes for little twinkling feet, a cheap football for stolid little legs, a pile of roller skates, a vacant lot for the expending of energies. Mended sweaters and outgrown coats. A man coming in at lamp-light time. That is all I ask except the right to dream—and the picture above the mantle of a flaming sunset.

Chapter 5
Desert 'Scape (1943)

Written in 1945. Story of a family journey from Riverside, CA to near Barstow, CA during World War II. Narrator, Erma Peirson (author), Engineer (husband Wilfred R. Peirson), The Air Reservist (son, James Peirson), Miss Muffett (daughter Doris (Peirson) Dye) and Young Bill (son Wilfred S. Peirson). Set in the Summer of 1943.

With daughter Doris in Riverside, CA before moving to the desert.

From Missouri to the Mojave

It took a war to bring us to the desert. Under normal world conditions, the Mojave, or any other desert, is the last place we would have chosen for a permanent residence. But the war is no respecter of places for persons. I've told myself and the Katzies a good many times that we can take it if the boys in service can take it. That was my proposition in those red hot August days when we first got here, the Katzies, Papa and I.

The Katzies, by way of introduction, are the two exceedingly normal offspring that make life lively and interesting for us. They followed, in the wake of the older child who is now in air service, and who was cut of straight and definite cloth from the time he looked out upon this world from philosophical baby eyes. The Katzies, eighteen months apart in time, and about two months in outlook, have kept us from getting old the while they have aged us with that outlook.

They've been called the Katzies time immemorial, the source of the nomenclature surely understood by every "well read" American of any age or era! At the time of this data, they are no longer Katzenjammers to the outside world, but as children never grow up to their parents, so they will probably be the Katzies for time immemorial to come, albeit one has graduated to her first formal and the other is a hardy boy scout!

Employment has a great deal to do with the hegira of any family. This is no less true in wartime when military affairs have a way of playing an ace hand even in the lives of civilians. And there is always the attending yen to keep the home fires burning under one roof. So, in these years of global conflict one was apt to be shuttled anywhere on the home front.

We Come to the Desert

In our own case, it was the sun's fire burning over one particular roof—after we got to the desert. For we were doomed—of all times of the year—to migrate to the Mojave in the sunniest of sunny months.

Desert 'Scape (1943)

Commemorative Katzenjammer Kids postage stamp. The Katzenjammer Kids is an American comic strip that ran from 1912 to 1949 by Rudolph Dirks and drawn by Harold H. Knerr. It debuted in 1897 in the American Humorist. It was the first cartoon to express dialogue speech balloons in comic characters.

We arrived, mercifully, in the evening of July 31st, 1943. The days that followed became a challenge. I say challenge, for that is what the desert was from the beginning for some of us.

In that beginning there was sun and heat, wind and tumbleweed. A space so vast, of rocks and sand and sky. On the desert there will always be sun and heat, so powerful, and winds, so mighty. And tumbleweed, huge and rolling when dry, tumbling one upon another, until still high and rolling, they are entangled and seem to lurch forward one giant sprite—then gone with the desert winds until impeded by a fence, or to end in the narrow walls of a ravine. The rocks are with us, too, to that end, and the sand is taken in our stride, literally as well as figuratively, for there is nothing else to stride over. And there will be to the end, bitter or sweet, the sky. Great, wide, spacious. Never the same.

Those first days of a desert summer—I'll never forget them. Not even when the fascination of the desert gravitates me to its wide-open spaces for an eon or two.

The head of the house, in his capacity as engineer, had been on the payroll of a desert military post for two years. He had started with the defense movement, and when total war raised medusa heads, and his camp had expanded, he was cheered on for that indefinite period called duration.

We, the family, had held the home post intact nearly two hundred miles "down below" during that time, living thrillingly in a lively military center that before the war had been one of the cultural centers of Southern California. Our engineer came home each weekend, going back to his desert spaces each Monday morning.

James, the Air Reservist   Doris, Miss Muffett

And then we, the family, were caught in the tight grip of the housing shortage during the second year of his "warjourn" as we chose to term his place of residence. We had the two children of high school age, and the young Air Reservist who had finished high school and was marking time until Uncle Sam's call and F.D.R.'s greetings should take him on his way to sky adventures.

Desert 'Scape (1943)

Houses were as scarce as butter, and much harder to find than the old needle in the haystack that had emerged to join the defense march in an all-out metal drive to make up for some of that scrap that went to bomb Pearl Harbor.

Getting a place to live in a military zone in wartime is not only a puzzle, but a progressive game, one in which all the rules are awry.

Someone wants a place to live. Not from wishes or personal wants, but from necessity. Perhaps it is a military family, or one of that prolific kind, army civilian, perhaps from across the continent. Nothing for rent. They must buy a place. The someone in the purchased home has to get out. All prospects for that party turn out to be mental mirages, and they in turn must purchase a home. Then they must ask someone to vacate, and another household is upset. Still nothing for rent, and another has to start purchasing. It goes on and on like the well worn-out brook of Tennyson's, making ripples on the sea of housing. Somewhere in that mazy wartime game we were side swiped.

The game was the perfect state of affairs known as a "vicious circle". A new collegiate dictionary, off-shoot of the honored Webster, gives as the definition of the "vicious circle", "a chain of circumstances constituting a situation in which the process of solving one difficulty creates a new problem involving increased difficulty in the original situation". This, in modern parlance, hit the housing situation square on the head—if a circle can hit squarely.

The large house we had lived in for years, and which was almost everything we wanted, was sold. The purchaser had sold his former home for profit and convenience and had to have possession. We couldn't get out, for there was nothing to rent—and we weren't ready to purchase. He was kind enough not to press the OPA privileges, and in return we promised to vacate as soon as school was out, "or as soon thereafter as we could find a place to move into."

We looked in vain. The ads in the papers for housing were yards long. Where once the landlord had trouble keeping his property rented, he now had mobs to combat to keep someone from taking over. So, the ads were no help. Neither were our friends, the real estate people. They were busy selling. The housing hunt became the twain that never met—the tenant and the next house. If one was "sold down the river" it was simply a case of the survival of the smartest, or a case of turning around and doing "thou likewise". Even the golden rule was of necessity out of vogue.

With us, we were not sold down the river, but out on the Mojave Desert. Sufficient unto the day of necessity, about the time the new landlord was cramped past endurance, and weary of living in the small trailer he had bought to domicile himself while we searched for living quarters, we found a house on the desert.

A young sergeant on the military outpost where The Engineer was "attached" was transferred to another post, a pawn in the Army's shuttle, and his family started to play the game. He'd passed the word to us and we were able to take over. It was nothing short of a miracle.

A truck was sent down from the desert to take our unworldly goods to the Mojave. The children and I were to motor up in a few days. There were last visits, goodbyes to say, last minute shopping. We were leaving all civilization! The children had a hundred places to go. A million things to do. It was like an emigration.

My friend Hallee arranged a last minute get together of choice friends for me the night before I left. After a gay little supper, replete with perfect viands, well rationed and planned, and much food for thought, also well rationed for they were gentle-folk, these gifted ones read some of their lovely poems of the desert. They made the desert sound so nice, something to look forward to with pleasant anticipation. Then afterwards we went to a late movie. It was a desert picture. That, without pre-arrangement, for we drove out to a little theater in an outlying village. [Possibly *Castle in the Desert*, a mystery movie starring Charlie Chan and set in the Mojave Desert.]

It was evening on a Saturday when we left. A flat tire delayed us en route, so we entered the Mojave in the darkness. The car went at a steady gait, whipping up an artificial wind to add to the cooling

Desert 'Scape (1943)

atmosphere that so strangely wraps the desert at night, regardless of the heat of the day.

We crossed Cajon Pass in velvet, dark depths. Cajon, meaning ox-like, on the trail of the old Spanish era. Darkness, studded with far away stars. There was no moon, and except for the stars, the blackness was deep. Now and then a train shot comet-like through the quiet spaces. It would be gone, and we were left to the swish of the tires, tired silence and the sleepy kids.

As we rolled through the dark fabric of the night, we saw, suddenly, a bright twinkling spot far to the distance. It seemed to be one perpetual wink. The lights scintillated and gleamed. It was like sparkling jewels set off in space.

The lights came from the Victorville Army Airfield, at Adelanto. There was no dim-out on the desert. It gave us a thrill to see the Base at night. We had been by there once many months before, in the daylight hours. At that time our country was not yet involved in the world fracas, except for defense measures and training purposes. I remembered having expressed myself feeling sorry for the fellows having to be set down so far from more exciting centers for their training. I imagine them, which was probably true, wanting to be nearer civilization, meaning cities. Now in the second year of our own participation in the global war, I know many of them were picnicking to what they have experienced since, for many fine fliers have gone from Victorville Field.

That is one of the great things the desert has done for an ungrateful nation, giving its great spaces for intense training for our armies of the air and ground. I say ungrateful nation, because as a nation, and as a people, we have never loved the desert. It has always been just something to get around, or across as quickly as possible, cursing, hurrying, hating, to reach the paradise of the Pacific Coast. A stumbling block to irk the journey.

People have cursed the desert since the days of the Spanish explorers. They have parched upon it. They have hated it. They have sweltered, hungered, become lost, died upon it. It was only there to try men's souls, to be forgotten except in moments of decided hatred when one remembered passage. Something that really wasn't worth a second thought, unless one were outlawed, like an old debt, to be forgotten. Something that the greatest stretch of imagination had trouble seeing in blossom.

Perhaps that has been part of the infinite plan. Perhaps it was made just so to wait for today. Today that shows the desert in a different role than ever it had been seen.

Crossing through the darkness, watching the shimmering lights at the airfield, I think I realized for the first time what the desert was doing for the war effort. That these great empty spaces, spared by nature from having throngs of people and industries, with room for thought and plans and training could have a part in the outcome of the future for the world. Perhaps they mean a future for the future, if one can see what I mean.

The lights of the air base went behind us and soon faded into the oblivion of the night. The tires continued to swish, and the wind whipped up pungent odors. Joshua trees loomed as vague outlines on either side of the highway. I knew that some units of that grotesque army that arched backwards from us held waxy, beautiful blossoms that told a story of a special life of moth and tree. The Joshuas, riddle of the desert, only native tree of the desert, faded into the mystery of the night, their escape a crazy, contorted way of growth, ugly, but interesting, fascinating. The moth that gives it life also kills it, by eating into its heart and causing a new lateral to shoot, stopping the old line of growth. No one has any record of when a Joshua will flower next, no one has any way of telling its age, for it has no dependable yearly ring to tell how old it is. It is stingy with its comfort, casts no shade. Even its beautiful blossoms are irony. Where the bloom comes, the limb stops growing, starting a new, contorted branch to start the cycle again. They tell me, these naturalists, that the Joshua is of the lily family. It does not seem possible. One thinks of daintiness, of reedy stems, of appealing lightness when thinking of the lily plant.

Desert 'Scape (1943)

Convoys passed us, going back to their base at Camp Haan, which vicinity we had left, the trucks filled with soldiers who had been on intensive training for anti-aircraft, bivouacking on the far fringes of Camp Irwin, bordering toward Death Valley.

An airplane flew overhead. On routine flight, perhaps, from the field we had just passed, a part of the training program. On military affairs, it could be.

I felt a tug at my heart. My flying reservist, sitting so calmy in the flying darkness, was probably tuned in to the rhythm of the motors in the sky. That was where he wanted to be. Not just going to the desert to mark time on some mere earthbound job.

More miles, and suddenly there was light. Light that almost blinded our eyes, so used to the dim-out of the city. Neon signs that sparkled like colored jewels. There was, we found, neither dim-out nor blackout on the desert. That gave one a feeling of security—and safeness that was almost guilty, thinking of what was happening in other countries. These were the first neon signs we had seen in so many months; it was like a revelation. To us the lights had come on again. A prayer went up it would not be too long before they were all over the world.

Barstow was just ahead. Then over the hill, through the brightly lighted desert outpost, across the Mojave River we had been following for so many miles in the darkness, seeing only massed outlines of trees at interspersed intervals. Then out to the little brick house the sergeant and his family had vacated.

We'd come home. For it was to be home for quite some time.

Perhaps for duration, we didn't know. The Engineer had said he would give us from three to six months to complain. Then, he prophesied, we would be just like everybody else—we would succumb to the fascination of the desert!

The Spaces

We hadn't heard the call of the desert, really. The desert, like a distracted mother, had gone out and dragged us in like so many naughty children whom she had found it easier to go after than to bother to call.

As we approached our spaces, the little house was ablaze with lights. I unsettled myself from the relaxation I had allowed myself to follow into, for well I knew what awaited me. I'd been following The Engineer for quite some years. There would be beds to arrange. Bites to eat must be unearthed.

The youngsters unscrambled themselves from suitcases and boxes and blankets, tumbled out upon the endless space of sand that was white and gleaming under the rays of the search light over the nether end of the brick.

As we had turned into the yard, (it proved, indeed, to be spaces!) we heard a mighty roar. Entering our desert domicile, we had to raise our voices to the highest pitch possible to be heard above a blitz. The desert cooler was in operation.

It was a homemade affair, for those heaven-sent commercial miracles of mechanism to change the condition of broiling atmosphere were almost a thing of the past. Definitely they were not for civilians, with military priority on the available supply. But it did the work, and it was no mean construction, for The Engineer knew his air conditioning. He had worked several evenings getting it ready to cool the house for us, and the climatic condition that prevailed went a long way in cheering me over the state of affairs the house was in.

Moving out of a seven-room affair, with each room of spacious dimensions, things seemed a bit crowded in the small four rooms, with literally everything in the middle of the floor. The time was to come when I would see for myself I had a real house, as desert houses went, and that it was as large as houses were usually built on the desert. Pretentiousness, I was also to learn, was not a part of the desert plan, either of Nature or by individuals.

But the refrigerator was going, too, and we started evacuations for the water pitcher and the glasses, which were somewhere in that conglomeration of cartons and orange crates. The Engineer had thoughtfully brought out a few groceries, and there was another

Desert 'Scape (1943)

scramble to dig for dishes and utensils. We compromised on cheese sandwiches, and opened a few cans of small sausages, and 'shades of desert rats', we found a can of beans. Some milk, already cooled in the refrigerator for The Engineer and the young folks, and our desert life began. As I looked around at the jumbled mass in my future kitchen, I was grateful for the lunch we had had at noon with my friend, the wife of an army captain in Riverside, and again at the tea hour after she had helped me with my last-minute packing of personal belongings we had kept for the last days' use. She had not only fortified me with morale but had fed the inner woman and dire hunger of offspring. I couldn't eat that evening—the jumble was too much for me.

We made beds all over The Spaces. (The site of our warjourn became known that early in the inhabitancy as "The Spaces".) The friend who had driven us up, and who was also a Camp Irwinite with The Engineer, slept on a pair of old springs outside. He would be up early and out to the post. Sleeping out under the stars, I was advised, was an ordinary thing on the desert in summer.

The house was meagerly furnished, and for the life of me I couldn't see why things should seem so crowded. We had brought but a few pieces of furniture to add to the too few furnished furnishings, and it had looked, on the trip up to inspect the place, as though life on The Spaces might be but a sort of camping experience. We brought a davenport and a couple of cots. There was a double bed in one bedroom, and another pair of old springs that we found we could make more or less (emphasis on the less) comfortable with pads until we could find time and the store to purchase something better. It had been impossible to find anyone with a van going that far away to bring out anything from the larger trading points. So, we had come prepared to have an "experience".

There was a round dining table, somewhat worse for the desert wear and air, and an electric range, that was a joy in the very thought of summer days. We had brought a couple of chests of drawers and an accumulation of radios, three in number, the washing machine and my desk and filing cabinet. The small mountains and peaks about the house, it seemed, were our "personal belongings".

By the time everyone but myself was tucked in for the night somewhere amid the cartons and boxes, and "Skippy", The Engineer's dog shadow had found his master was going to stay, too, and not go to camp that night, so curled up on the floor, I gave an exhausted sigh and went outside to take another look at the desert at night.

There was a stillness over everything. It seemed strange without neighbors next door. For a long time, I was going to miss knowing when my neighbors came home at night with no slamming doors or windows or calls from departing cars to awaken me. I would discover some evening what it was like when there was no footfall on a porch to tell me someone was coming. We were about two miles out in the country, with neighbors a few "acres" away.

Barstow was built in two places. The old part of town, down along the river bottom, and the newer part on the hillsides. The lights of the town were across from us, and they flirted gaily as I stood by the athel trees to look at our new world. For so long I'd seen no lights shining except from next door, or across the street, partly shuttered out because of war regulations, or the dimmed-out streets of Riverside, that it seemed I was looking on a carnival of lights.

All the time I lived on The Spaces those lights were like jewels to me. And I thought so often of the pity of the places where lights had been out for so long, and I knew what a happy time it was going to be "when the lights go on all over the world".

I've seen the lights of Barstow in the density of the blackest of nights, through a moonlight world, in the gray of the river mists and the smoky darkness of early winter mornings. They never failed to intrigue me. Barstow was always the plaque, the lights were the gems. The plaque would change colors, but the jewels were the same bright things: gold, red, green and blue.

Desert 'Scape (1943)

Postcard of the Beacon Tavern in Barstow.

A gorgeous red sign from an oil and gasoline station tapered high into the night, and the wide lighted one of the Beacon Tavern gave the little town its citified look as I gazed across the river.

Off far away on a high peak, a bright light turned on and off at intervals as regularly as a mechanical wink. I figured it was a beacon for air travelers. And I was glad for such things, thinking of my air-minded boy asleep inside.

The stillness would last quietly, and then there would be a rumble as cars down in the older part of town were coupled, or as trains shrilled out into the deep, far spaces. Barstow is a railroad division point, a place of importance, really, making it more than a desert outpost. It is a connecting link with the outer world.

I looked at the little, square, boxlike house. It seemed so unfinished, as it was, without porches. I was to learn the little house itself had a story. But now, it just looked tired, as I was. And it never looked any different. It seemed to squat there under the high feathery athel trees. The only time I ever really liked the house was when we drove in at night and the lights had been left on. Then it seemed cheery, and one felt a warm feeling of welcome.

I think a porchless house has a terribly let-down look, especially if it is square and low and there is no landscaping to set it off properly. Goodness knows, there is plenty of landscaping around the little brick, but there is also too much stretch, and nothing in proportion.

A breeze came up from out of the nowhere, and the tall trees shushed a sleeping world with their swishing sound. I felt sleepy, too. It was nearly midnight on Saturday, July 31st.

I thought I would leave the desert night to its mystery, the little brick to its weariness, and went inside with my own. The bed would feel good, I knew, even if the casters were gone and the springs and mattress were all but on the floor. After shooting several hundred mosquitoes, not to speak of numerous insects whose acquaintance I'd never met before, nor dreamed could exist in such quantities, I fell, desert-tired, into the low bed. With the blitz turned off, the air was not so pleasant, but it was something to be able to hear my own thoughts.

Before I knew it, it was another day, and I started a new life.

Patterns

Somehow, there wasn't much strangeness after a while, and we found we were more or less settled into a new scheme of life on the desert. One got used to the great silence of vast spaces. The bright, glaring sky of noonday was somehow lived through. The life of the city began to seem as though it had never been a reality, but something dreamed of, visited perhaps, but no longer, surely, a part of our being.

Mornings were lovely. Getting up was a reward for living on the desert. The colors of a desert dawn! No words fully and justifiably express or describe them. For an hour after getting up time, the beauty came slowly, surely, and full of changing colors. Suddenly, a sun burst shot itself through that maze of diversified colors, and the day had begun.

Desert 'Scape (1943)

By noon the sun was a fury, hiding nothing in its scalding attempt to wither every person, plant, drop of water. On into a lazy afternoon, when the inside of the house was far, far better than any activity, no matter how dull life could be inside.

But the evenings were bound to come. Evening, with its shadows and reflected glory, dying, in the far horizons with pictures no mortal can ever hope to paint. The peace of a summer desert night, when cooling breezes come up as if the world was remorseful for having treated us so harshly with its burning sun and tearing, oven-winds.

Young Bill started a brood of chickens at The Spaces along with his other animal pals.

As we took up our new life on the desert, we found plenty to do. It was the promised land for Young Bill, then a farmer at heart and loves all outdoor things. He seemed blessed with all the inheritance of the pioneers and homesteaders on both sides of the family tree. He took to the wide-open spaces, the sand and the sun like a duck to water. His butter-colored hair turned to the color of the sun, and his very fair skin, after a few burnings, took on its first permanent tan. His eyes, already of depths of blue like the summer skies, twinkled in his enjoyment of his brand-new life.

Miss Muffett, though, had to adjust herself. She was going to miss her parties and her pals, and for a few weeks, life was a rather strenuous way of living just getting adjusted to country life on the desert. The flying reservist wasn't much concerned either way. He knew what was ahead of him. He had trips to make back and forth to March Field for physicals and examinations. He had his little marking time job at Camp Irwin to keep occupied until he was called into active participation with the army.

I, the Mama, had come up to help keep the home ties all in one spot for the short time our flier would be home. I didn't think I could stand the household split three ways. It was going to be rather tough when the day came for the eighteen-year-old to make the first break in the ties. A challenge beside the desert was facing me. But it was war, and I tried to console myself, all through the hot weeks of summer that brought me nearer to the birthday [September 5th], that we were better off than millions of others. We were so safe, we who stayed at home. But there were times when I thought of the future desert in my heart when my first born would be gone, and the spirit would grow weak along with the flesh.

But finally, life dissolved itself into a pattern, and I was intrigued in spite of my future worries.

At the end of the day, when the evening meal was over, we would either "stack" the dishes, or wash and rinse them and pile them into the dish drainer and one by one drift to the front of The Spaces to sit and watch the sky and landscape pictures. An old wicker rocker that "went with the place" seemed to belong to me. I always sat in it, with a pad of paper in my lap and a pencil in my hand. It seemed a crying shame not to start putting down some of the wonders of the desert evening on paper. But I usually ended up just watching it, feeling it.

As each day went by, I would wonder how I was ever going to stand it to the end, how I could ever bear another one of such heat, and such monotony of living. Too hot outside to stay out for any time. Too hot to be in any part of the house except where the blitz roared on. Life, when home, took on the semblance of exile. Just staying in one room seemed to do something to my active soul.

But with the dropping of the sun, the world changed entirely. We began to live, then. But we found we were living quietly. There was a satisfaction about just sitting under the mellowed skies, watching the tall trees sway in the slightest breeze that come up with the going down of the sun. The sky became a darker blue, giving way gradually, strangely invisibly, to a silver shade. Stars snapped into place like turning on the lights of a Christmas tree. They seemed, too, so close to earth. We, town saturated, were almost breathless at being able to see them. Nothing between us and the canopy of the heavens. I wondered often when I had last seen stars. I couldn't remember.

For a long time, I fretted because there was no grass under our feet. I wanted the youngsters to lie down next to the earth, to look directly at the stars. There is something about doing that which seems to build some deeper meaning into one's soul. But the dust was too thick for that, and there was always the fear of rattlesnakes—which even grass would not have changed.

For diversion, we would throw small stones for Skippy, the fox terrier. He took on the look of a small kangaroo as he hopped over the tumbleweed, whirled quickly, sniffing for the special rock thrown. He would never bring another, not if it took him fifteen minutes to search for it.

The soldiers at camp, where Skippy spent every day with The Engineer, passed their idle hours playing with him. He had been there two years before we went desertward, too, when The Engineer only came home on weekends with him. Skippy took it as a matter of course that we should spend our hours, idle and otherwise, tossing a rock, or some equivalent, for him to retrieve. If we spoke gently, or spoke at all, he went for a rock or stick. If indoors, it would be a marble, or anything from a fruit jar lid to a pin.

The Engineer with Skippy.

When we were fortunate enough to find single beds for the boys, we brought out the old wire folding cot and the old bed springs, to place on the front of The Spaces. We placed the springs on top of the one we had dragged up from the back of the place and put one on the other. We spread an army blanket over it, and at least two of us could lie there and look straight at the stars, with someone usually sprawled on the cot.

Much as it meant to be able to be outside and relax in the blessed coolness of the desert evening, I never once lay down on the spring bed without a feeling of insecurity, for I knew the snakes came out at night when the earth was cooled. I've been told, and think it is true, that snakes will live less than an hour if they stay out in the sun during the hottest part of the day. I loved to walk off an evening. I missed the lighted avenues to take my habitual evening walk. I wanted to start out across The Spaces and walk toward the hills. But to do so would court the attention of scared rattlers. I tried walking up and down the paved road in front of The Spaces but was afraid to go far with the darkness coming on. All that first summer I worried about Bill being outside, for he was everywhere on foot and on his bike. But

Desert 'Scape (1943)

we saw nary a snake on The Spaces in the eleven months we were privileged to stay there!

We could see the trees that lined the Mojave River. We were perhaps a half mile from the riverbed that curved and turned like a mighty snake. Although there was no water there, on top, the trees were green all summer. I guess I was there for several months before I took an interest in that sandy, curving, waterless riverbed. By and by I began to find out things about my desert—and the strangest thing of all was the river that ran through the desert underground for more than ninety miles.

When evening comes the tree line of this river makes a lovely break in the bend. The lights would come on and the whole hillside was twinkling and beautiful. Much more beautiful to us, out on The Spaces, than it would have been in town where the majority of the houses were small, the yards allotted.

But the lights of town spelt life. Little homes where people were crowded, now as never before, with the housing shortage what it was, and with people coming in throngs to work on the military installations, and the fast-growing railroad business, which has always been a factor in Barstow.

We proved a busy family as the months went by. Had we not been, I fear before the summer was over we would have taken to the road and proved ourselves vulnerable. It was the beautiful evenings, and the blitz, that saved that first summer for us. We seldom listened to the radio in an evening. Usually we were outside, but if inside, we couldn't have it and the blitz too. We compromised, without exception, for the air cooler. Even though the breeze came up in the evening, the house would not be cool, for the heat of the day seemed locked within the walls.

The Engineer, of course, was grooved into his work. I finally went to work on an army post ten miles away. The Air Reservist went with The Engineer and Skippy. They went early, leaving the house at seven to catch the army truck that took them to work. The first five months I worked, I rode with individuals that came by for me. The ride in the morning was lovely, into the east. But the homeward trip was of cooking temperature.

My morning pattern evolved by the winter. I was off the beaten trail by from a half to three quarters of a mile, so I had to walk that distance to catch the bus. The Engineer and Skippy would be on their way a full half hour before I left. I would call the two Katzies, hoping they wouldn't go back to sleep. I would wrap up in my muffler, head scarf, wool coat, and an extra pair of ankle socks over my rayons and start down the road to meet the sunrise.

One morning the frost was so thick I thought I must be transferred to some other place. My world of the desert was like something on an embossed Christmas card. A tan colored stucco house stood by the side of the road where my road made the junction with the highway to Yermo. A wire fence enclosed the neat yard. Small trees lined the fence, and a hardy vine curled along the trim latticed wire mesh. The whole thing from the winter bared ground to the wire mesh looked as though silver paint had been sprayed daintily over it all. A coat of frost on the roof set the buff stucco into etched outlines.

Young Bill, the pioneer soul, took care of The Spaces, tried his hand at a garden, adopted a couple of yellow kittens, and for once had all the room he wanted to play in. Not quite old enough to be a young man, and still not a little boy, he was content to romp with his dog, start a brood of chickens, hike around the desert, and ride his bike.

Bookends, Young Bill's yellow cats. Thomas on the left and Little Goldilocks on the right.

Desert 'Scape (1943)

The kittens were his most precious possessions. He has a perspective soul. One evening he called me into the living room.

"Come and see the bookends, Mother."

I walked into the room where the blitz was in full control, wondering where the kid had found bookends. On a couch, below the blitz, lay the yellow cats, rump to rump, heads pointing in different directions, but with the same pose and angle, still and motionless, fluffy tails curled precisely alike around their bodies, looking for all the world like two painted composition bookends. The cats were called the Bookends for most of their life with us.

Little Goldilocks, who presented us with babies several times, became a wonderful hunter. She was forever bringing up mice from the feed room, and lizards were easily caught, and a common diet. She was always a hustler, but the other one, christened Thomas A. (Alley)—Goldilocks, strangely, was long haired—Thomas was just a big overgrown, old pet, not worth a darn out to sing.

The Engineer, with his interesting hobby of cooking carried me through many a hot and tiring day by his help in the kitchen. Bill completely took over the outside, cleaning The Spaces of years of tin cans and dried tumbleweed. He could not grow grass, for the well would have given up the ghost and broken its last rusty joint in a day when spare parts were impossible to get. His attempts to have a garden failed, for it was cooked by the sun and nibbled by the rabbits and proved a dying dream for the little fellow who wanted his Victory Garden so much.

Laundry became a problem. In fact, because I worked on the post, I had to take care of that on a Sunday. A laundress was out of the question—and the laundry in town that first year wouldn't take any except military. When they loosened up to take civilian laundry, it would be weeks before they were returned. So, there was no recourse but drag the washer into the house and go after it. There were no set-in tubs in the little brick house, so I had it the hard way. Water was transferred into the machine by a length of hose from the tap at the sink. The rinsing usually was done a few pieces at a time in the dish pan. In summer, they were dry almost before they were pinned to the line. But the desert has its extremes and there were times that first winter when they almost froze on the line before I got them pinned.

The Engineer with Skippy and Tray at The Spaces

When the halfhearted laundry was finished, it was amazing what I found in the bottom of my empty Easy. I vow a goodly portion of the desert was there. How that old machine ever withstood the sand that went through its mechanism is still beyond me. Now, at this writing, two years after I brought it to the desert, it is still going strong, with never a break or bit of repair. Now there's a plug for the washing machine firm, and I should get a bonus!

Our meals those first months resolved themselves into simple affairs. There was little time or inclination for baking. I set a simpler table than I had ever done in all my housekeeping years. In the first place the shortage and rationing of food on the desert was greater than down below [Riverside]. What was available was purchased by the ladies who did not work on the posts or for the railroad. By the time we reached town, after gathering the family together, there was little left to choose from, especially in the way of meat. We got it catch as catch can. Fortunately for our meat appetites, we had our own chickens and eggs.

Baking was not frequent because of the sugar angle. We could get a nice pie, or rolls if we got into town in time, but the bakery issued no cakes. The sugar and shortening shortage caused that. There were times when the one bakery closed for a few days at a time because of the shortages.

So, time and rationing put a damper on the sweets. But in spite of the fact we had a less varied diet, and it was boiled down to essentials, we all thrived. The youngsters grew up and I grew in width. I've never quite understood why all of a sudden, coming to the desert where living was harsh, and food was scarcer and less rich that I started growing. It wasn't relaxation, it wasn't rich foods, and it wasn't lack of exercise. I can only figure that there is something in the air, or water minerals. Elixir of some sort breathed in from the great unpolluted spaces may have been a factor. From a mere one hundred five pounds I jumped in two years' time to at least twenty-five pounds more. I have noticed a great proportion of fat women on the desert. More of them than men in comparison.

By the first of November, when the hot days were receding from the desert, the great break came when the young reservist left for his training. He was glad to get into the branch he had chosen, and there was some small comfort in his going. But choosing as he did, with the thrill and hopes of conquering the air, we felt a portion of his pride. Yet I never see a plane dart across the skies, or hear one throbbing, that it does not take on a deep meaning.

I still feel sometimes he must be just in the other room, and I find myself after nearly two years since his departure starting to want to tell him something. All the time I lived on The Spaces, after his going, I missed him most. It seemed he was still there. When the day came and we had to move, I lost the feeling he was "just in the other room". But I find myself feeling he is somewhere not too far, and I tuck things back into my memory to tell him on paper.

That first year he was away, and it got too bad, I would cut out across The Spaces and stand on a knoll, look around at the great world of my desert 'scape. The hills were so staunch, and they had stood there, blistering through eons of scorching sun. I looked out across the spaces that are so wide, so beckoning, so serene. Something settled the grief and unrest at having my first born go out of the home, to face his adventure in the skies.

Mornings

This whole volume could be devoted to telling of desert skies, and still justice could not be done to the subject. The picture is constantly changing. I have stood in the kitchen on The Spaces and looked out the double windows, watching the dawn break. I have strained mentally to note the split second when a rose tint became an orchid hue, to quickly turn into blue, and at the blink of an eyelid appear some strange shade of green. I was never able to note the break—or the time of the transition of colors, it was done so quickly, yet never any seeming hurry about it. It came so gradually, yet so quickly. The Engineer expressed it as a time of slow fastness. I think that is good enough.

In pre-desert days I often pondered over the expression about skies holding pictures no artist could paint. In my ignorance of painting and in lack of understanding of the miracles in the skies, I thought it was just a pretty expression. I ponder no more. Before an artist can assemble, or mix his colors, the picture changes, leaving an amazing wonder at what had been, the pattern lost in the new wonder of an entirely different array of colors and sky pictures.

I have walked into a winter sunrise feeling as though I were not of earth. Colors that heralded the sun splashed across the eastern sky. Some mornings un-nameable hues greeted me on my way eastward to meet the army bus. Other times it seemed that the rainbow had crumpled to a heap in one corner of the world.

Desert 'Scape (1943)

I have trekked down the highway when the first tints of dawn streaked through the still gray sky like sharp points of colored steel. There have been mornings when the sky was a riot of colors. They changed so fast, so gaily, and so softly I could only compare them to gaily dressed fairies, dashing rakishly and rapidly behind one another, detecting no feature of fact or form.

There have been mornings when the skies were darkly hovering between the night and the dawn, and the sudden onslaught of color in the east was a fanfare of radiance, brightness and glory. One could almost imagine a jeweled Ferris Wheel hanging tremblingly in the east.

There was one morning when all I could see before me was a purple mist. It excluded any touch of red or pink, blues or ambers. What color might have been behind that mist veil that lingered over the breathless world, I could not tell. The purple billow receded in time, but as I watched it, I could not tell what instant I saw it, and what it looked like as it became something else. When it left, I could not tell. It was a beautiful dream.

I have seen the east of a morning a solid blue, a dark cast at first; on a second look, a pure turquoise, so, still so beautiful and so serene that I was at peace with the universe, and so grateful for the privilege of just being there to look at a sunrise.

Scarcely a winter morning as I walked out from The Spaces but what I wanted to start singing, "Oh, beautiful for spacious skies." And sometimes I did—if not verbally, the strain of the melody went rhythmically through my mind. I could not help but wonder how a world with such beauties could be at war.

The steel silver of a desert dawn! The changing, delicate hues that clothe the sky, the radiance of the sun-hurst that follows. There is nothing in all the world like it.

So much of the desert I have not liked. There have been times when it irked me just to look at the heat ripples in the air. When I felt another day of oven-heat winds would slay me. When the routine of duties, the sameness of life, and surroundings almost got me down and out, but always there was enough sky beauty to off-set the drab things.

Some mornings, although it was seven-thirty, the moon was still high, vying in its serene, cold beauty and its graceful swing, the hurrying riot in the east. My neck took many a twisting trying to see the whole dome of the heavens at once. There was so much peace and quiet out there in the still of the morning. I wouldn't have missed those walks for the price of plenty of tires and gas coupons. The town of Barstow was off to my right, and I gradually left it behind me, but I turned often to watch the lights that blinked out gradually as I walked back into The Spaces.

Barstow was a railroad town, and I could hear the bumping of the trains, a whistle that told of a departing train, and the smoke rose high into the morning air. During the deep winter weeks, the beacon light on a far-off hill was still blinking its helpful gleam as I stood on the junction waiting. Every morning the picture was new, and I could tell why no painter had ever been able to paint the perfect picture of the sunrise. It was because it changed too fast for the colors, had they been made of the right shades, to be reached and put on the canvas, and the scene was ever different morning after morning. I have seen colors I could not name, colors only the Master Painter could perfect.

The shadows cast over the hills, the tree line along the river, the slowly awakening valley were all one could ask for beauty and a start for the day. I shall never forget the wall of silver white mist, scalloped and graceful, that followed the bend of the snaky Mojave River one morning, completely shutting from my sight the trees and hills with at one thin place in that misty wall, a ghostly outline of a windmill showing.

The strange thing, after absorbing all that beauty, was that I cannot recall any particular pattern in the sky. The change was always so fleeting, each new cast so beautiful it pushed the definiteness of the pattern from my memory. So many sunrises, all so different, so quickly changing to something else again, it was too much for a

Desert 'Scape (1943)

mere mortal to register. But the subconscious has something of it left; appreciation for beauty; a memory of morning clouds billowing ahead; golden bursts of light accepting rosy tints, stern, dark shades peering over the rim of hills to clear the coast for the burst of glory of rain¬bow hues to be ushered in. Smoke wreathing around a hill to make a frame, a shrill shriek from an engine to give life to that was so still, the lights of the town blinking out as though in shame at trying to compete with such natural, rushing beauty.

Spring dawns, not quite so vigorous, steal over the world at an earlier hour. Their act of daring and defiance seems to say, "I came late, all winter, to humor you. Now, lazy souls, get up if you want to meet me. I'm quite gay, really. It might be worth your while."

And worth one's while it is, to emerge from sleep a bit earlier in order to see what the morning of a spring dawn can be. The colors do not seem so noisy, the dawn comes less slowly, with less sky drama. Spring is short, and there is much work to do. The flowers will soon want to peer above their shallow beds. They are not the type that come slowly through the soil, from deep beds. They have no roots, really, they sleep close to the surface of the earth, sad the hot spring suns pull them up rapidly, and almost at once, from their sandy beds.

Sunsets

Then come the sunset hours. At evening, the world was clothed in beauty for me. While we were on The Spaces, it was an evening ritual to go outside and watch the sun sink in the west over the line of hills. The next thing was to turn and look at the eastern range that held all the reflected glory of the sunset. The Calico mountains ran away to the left, the Newberries to the right as I stood in the yard of The Spaces. They would be pink for a time with the reflected glory, then with the falling light they turned that glorious shade of deep blue that is so beautiful on a mountain range. The road to Yermo ran east from The Spaces, and as night fell, the lights of cars coming down the hill from the Yermo road was like a lighted, moving lantern. Looking off beyond the town of Barstow, there were the lights of the Marine

Supply Base, twinkling in one spot in a drop in the terrain. On beyond that, the road that led to the Douglas Modification Center, and which later became an army airport, was almost a constant moving of lights, crawling along over the hill.

```
Erma Peirson      Editorial clerk

Aug. 1943 to Dec. 1944      Clerk, Yermo Holding and Reconsignment Point
                                   Yermo, California (now part of
   Started at GS 2 and left as GS 4  Marine Depot of Supplies, Barstow
                                   are).
                                   Transportation Corps, USA.
   Supervisor: Capt. Walter P. Chambers

Description of duties:  In charge of indexing, making chages, of
Army Regulations, circular letters, directives, and accumulating
same into library.  In charge of all Standard and Civil Service
Forms, keeping stock replenished by requisitions from Ogden Depot.
Typing and filing, miscellaneous.

Had charge of General Supplies warehouse overseeing two enlisted
men for distribution of office supplies to Point offices.  Requisition-
ed stock.  Also kept complete inventory of all Point property,
making Tally-in and Tally-out sheets for all incoming and outgoing
officers for property for which they were responsible.  Made
requisitions for all property used on Point, and for supplies
prepared for shipping overseas.  Assisted as Property Supply Clerk
and various duties connected with Office of Station Quartermaster.
During the year and one-half employed there went from one job to
another as vacancies occured  in office and continued in charge of
position vacated for another to traing new girls.

Left position because moved to another part of area and had no
transportation, so sought employment more conveniently located
and with plans for Public Relations work in offing at Daggett.
```

Excerpt from 1952 resume

When we drove home from town where we all met, the sky in the west was ablaze with colors too beautiful to call and patterns too lovely for description. Little rugged Bill was usually outside when the sun was in its glory. Were I home and in the house at the hour when all beauty lovers should be outside, and an especially beautiful sunset occurred, he would come calling eagerly for me to come out and see the sky. Bill and I lived for the evenings, winter or summer, and the sunrises always followed the night.

One evening as we came home to The Spaces from town, we saw a rainbow. We had seen many in our months there, but this one seemed something sent directly from heaven to give us a special

Desert 'Scape (1943)

one for beauty-memories. As we left the bridge across the river, and turned on Highway 466 to reach The Spaces, in about a quarter of a mile, the rainbow arched over the desert, seeming to take in the whole world. I have never seen so large a rainbow. The colors were very distinct and seemed close to earth. The right-hand end of the bow was off across town toward the Marine Base, but the left-hand end fell directly to the earth and lay in green and yellow stripes on the hills in back of our place. The air was so still, so mellow from the evening shades, and the arc so huge and colorful that something seemed to well up inside me and almost choke me with the beauty of the bow. I asked The Engineer to let me out of the car. I wanted to walk on home and see the bow as long as I could. Bill got out with me, and we went home slowly, and stopped often to peer upward at it.

Something about that rainbow arching over our desert valley meant a lot to both of us. There was a throb of beauty in the whole evening. The hills would always hold something of the bright hues it gave them for such a short time. The high athel trees swished over the brick. The dogs came to meet us. The lights went on in the little brick. We crossed the sandy yard and went inside.

Chapter 6
Desert Fascinates (1948)

Published in the China Lake Naval Ordnance Test Station Rocketeer on October 27, 1948, as part of the Desert Scrapbook series. Erma and family take a road trip from China Lake, CA to Los Angeles.

Representative of the desert landscape in part, is this photo of the Sand Dunes of Death Valley. During a wind storm these dunes change shape and place, as the fine sand is whirled about. (Burton Frasher Sr.)

Whenever we return from an eventful weekend in town, we are amazed in retrospect at the many and diversified things we have accomplished in so short a time—and how glad we are to be back on the desert.

Sailing through the Naval Ordnance Test Station (NOTS) main gate on schedule (the car serviced the night before) we felt a sense of release. We'd felt so pent up for so long; felt so isolated behind our fence; so out of things here on the wide-open spaces.

But we're on our way out and the miles fly swiftly under us as we contentedly take for granted the heavenly blue desert skies. Clipping through the golden air that is so vibrant and exhilarating, wings are attached to the spirits and dull care is left on the wasteland.

We scarcely note the receding line of the mighty Sierra that towers sentinel-like over our fringe of the great Mojave Desert. Passing through squatty little desert hamlets, there is a vital anticipation of tall buildings in town; of throbbing, pulsing crowds on metropolitan streets. In amazement we note the many cars going in the opposite direction.

Barren hills, upon which rest mellowed dark shadows of soaring clouds, fail to find a spark in the desert weary breast. Looking casually at them, it is easy to forget that those somber knolls and peaks had helped to make western history as their vitals lured miners and prospectors. Tales of bandits had no interest. Ridiculous figures of tons and dollars which they spitted out in ore, that helped to build our western empire, seem impossible, and no longer of interest.

There is an increasing wonder within us as to why people stay upon the desert stretches. The small, tree-spotted plots off at the base of brown, serene hills beyond the highway seem like only a picture. Could we possibly have trudged through heavy sand and graveled washes to see what made it look so enticing? Surely, no one in his right mind could be contented to live out there with only wild sage, bunch grass or creosote to encompass the eye. The low, weathered buildings certainly cannot hold content and interest for anyone.

Desert Fascinates (1948)

The wind raises a whirlpool of fine sand on a lonely gap of desert waste where only sere dwarfed vegetation raises pitiful heads. (We have forgotten the riotous wildflower garden of spring, already.) Too, we remember lonely walks toward the desert horizon, and we know there are places where winter rains have washed away the small plant life of the rugged ravines. Now only small pebbles gleam in the sunshine, with rainbow colors reflecting every glimmer.

The memory of bright spring days, when the washes were lined with tiny gold mats, as a ceramic bowl is lined with artful figures, brings a small moment of nostalgia. But that is only a wisp in memory, now, for the bright gardens of the southland are just ahead.

The rapid transit from one world to another is so gradual and casual; it is difficult to know just where the desert ends and the "other world" begins. The line of demarcation is pretty fine, with science and industry fast invading the desert wilderness.

The metropolitan area approaches and it is a far-fetched idea to absorb the fact that Southern California was once a desert, too.

But vast green lands where parks have been laid out; rolling golf links; huge tree-bounded estates, with magnificent buildings; small, lush lawns, with well-kept, year-round green hedges, and roses in bloom hanging over walls, greet us. Blossoming, exotic vines climbing over pleasing architectural structures are a welcome vision.

We are in the city of angels, and trillions of flowers, a million people, and great activity is now ours. Dull hours are gone for all time. We began to feel quite cosmopolitan. The crowds make our pulses quicken. The great, modern stores beckon with their wares. We're seeing life again amid the maelstrom of people. The dizzy feeling we have is just excitement, interest and joy.

We will spend the afternoon shopping, or at a ball game; browse through a museum or attend a wedding, a reception, a dinner, or a high-priced, famous show. It's been years since we've lived in such a manner. We see familiar faces in a store where we didn't expect to be recognized, and strangely, we are excited when we see a desert friend in a restaurant. We call on old friends who think we have come home from a land "far distant", and we meditate a second on why it is farther to the desert than away from it. The whole city, perhaps the whole southern area, seems to be on parade. For two days we kept going, crowding every moment to the fullest.

But we've grown a little weary of crowds and hurry, and we look at our purchases, at our tired faces and wonder why we thought we were busy back on the desert, and there runs through our minds the meetings, the reports, the parties, the lectures, our work—all the things we did "at home" which we thought we would escape when we left for the desert.

The desert fascinates many who find peace, content and its interest.

Chapter 7
Television: The One-Eyed Monster (1949)

Written in the mid-1950s and set in 1949. Erma reflecting on home life changes with emerging technology.

My reaction to our first television set in 1949.

From Missouri to the Mojave

Television is here to stay. Most definitely it is here to stay in my living room. Personally, I took the coming of television in my stride, as I have all the inventions and conveniences of this modem age, but never have I run up against anything inanimate that I could liken to a tyrant.

My home was peaceful at one time. We had a large living room into which many friends came to chat, play cards, and enjoy coffee and cake. The friendliness of the living room was like something live and vital. The sun shone through the many windows during the day and the lighted lamps made it cozy at night.

When friends call NOW, we have to sit and watch the television. They either leave to come no more or fall right in with the other members of the family and glue themselves to the tyrant. I, who cling to the old pattern of friendliness, am beginning to cry, "Oh, where are the friends of yesteryear?"

I am not against television. I could enjoy it within reason. But there are too many things to be done to give all one's waking hours to it.

The television is at the end of the living room where one must pass going to and from the bedroom, bath, kitchen and outside. When I pass, or for some reason pause, in front of the machine, friend husband bawls out, "Get out of the way." When someone comes in to visit and I've been quiet so long I'm hungry to hear a human voice (outside of the television) he yaps out again, "Well, let's listen to the television."

The blinds are pulled during the day to keep the light out and at night the lights are turned off. It is like being in a dungeon. I have been forced to buy a flashlight and go around in the evening like Diogenes of old, hunting for books, or whatever I might need or want. Don't dare turn on a light or I'm bawled out again with remarks like, "I can't see the picture."

When the young folks are home weekends, my troubles are quadrupled. Can I get help for anything in the house? No. The answers

Television: The One-Eyed Monster (1949)

to my requests go like this, "Oh, I've just got to see this program!" or "Just stack the dishes, Mom, I'll do them after Jack Benny is over."

The living room furniture is completely changed about the room. The couch at the farthest point so all can see well. The desk is moved and the cat's favorite perch is ruined, as he is set in his ways and the desk is not his throne in any other spot. The dog goes around like a lost soul because her couch is occupied.

There is no end to the problems that are piling up. I can't vacuum because I am told it is too noisy. House stays dirty. Can't use the sewing machine. Interferes with reception. Can't use cake mixer. Bothers reception. We're hungry. Can't iron. Makes static. Clothes are wrinkled.

I have been relegated to one of the back rooms in order to escape the television every waking moment. I do my writing there (thank goodness my typewriter isn't electric, or I would have to stop that too). I hope to have the telephone moved in also. Talking on it in the living room interferes with those who watch the television. Sometimes some member of the family deigns to open the door and look in to see if I have evaporated. I simply glare them out.

Family meals are a thing of the past. The daughter-in-law brought up, of all things, television tables. I think I'll rent the dining room out.

From out of all the turmoil of television in my home, I am convinced all homes to be built in the future and all homes of the present should have a television room.

I wonder what state I would be in if I were living in a two- or three-room house with no place to escape to and retain my sanity. I'd probably succumb to the watching of the television. I probably will anyway.

Erma (Patterson) Peirson Extended Biography

As this book is a collection of stories of her life, this biography has been extended to cover her immediate family who shaped her life.

Patterson Ancestry

The Patterson surname originates from Scotland. It results from the name Patrick, where Patrick's son is given the last name of "Patterson".

Erma's father was George Washington Patterson. George's father, Abraham, was from England whereas his mother, Mary's ancestry was from Germany.

The surname Marlow derives from the place in Buckinghamshire on the Thames in old England for a "mere" lake or boggy area after a lake or pool of water has drained.

George Washington Patterson's wife, Erma's mother, Martha Ann (Marlow), came from multiple generations in America. Her parents, Issac Marlow and Almira (Palmer) Marlow, lived in Illinois. They later moved to Nebraska and settled in Missouri. Almira was the second cousin of Confederate General, Robert E. Lee. There is also a family connection from the Palmers to Mary (Todd) Lincoln on the Todd side of her family.

Erma Mae Patterson

1899 Sisters Ruby, Erma, Almeda; 1910s Sunday dress;
1915 Country School Teacher

Born January 27, 1891, in Cobb, St. Clair County, Missouri, Erma Mae Patterson spent her childhood there. She was the middle child and had two sisters, Ruby (1890) and Almeda (1896).

Ruby married Dan Hungerford in 1913 and had three children, Dan - aka Jake (1916), Jerry (1923) and Patty (1924).

Almeda married Edward Davis and gave birth to Almeda "Jean" Davis on March 16, 1917, in Chowchilla, CA. Sadly, a week later Almeda died from complications due to childbirth. Ruby took the newborn into her home even though she had a six month old, and raised the little girl. Jean's father and step-mother took over raising Jean when she turned 12.

Ruby was a wonderful artist. She would paint objects, such as seashells and small boxes along with formal wall paintings. She was quite the character and always made people laugh.

Erma graduated from High School in Osceola, Missouri in 1908 and attended an extra year to get her teaching training. In the summer of 1909, after her father's unexpected passing, her mother, Martha Patterson, moved with her three daughters to Nebraska to be near her mother's relatives. Erma got her first job, working for the Republican, a local newspaper in Aurora, Nebraska.

Beginning in 1910, she taught in a number of elementary schools across five different states: Nebraska, Colorado, Wyoming, California, and Nevada. Several of those teaching stints were in one-room schoolhouses. Whenever she moved to a new state she was required to take an examination to qualify to teach there. During her time living in California, she took about a one-year break from teaching to work at the San Joaquin Light and Power as a clerk and cashier.

In December 1918, Erma came down with the Spanish Flu. It took her four months to recover, and she was able to return to teaching in March 1919 in Fallon, Nevada.

With the First World War underway, Erma decided to pen some patriotic songs to support the war effort and get them published. She would write a "Poem Song" and send it to a music company in Chicago and they would get a musician to write the accompanying music.

She submitted many titles for review and would have to pay the musician. In 1919, she got copyrights for three songs, "Our Uncle Sammy", "The Star of Gold" and "We Made the Kaiser Rally to Red, White and Blue".

She settled in Madera County, California in 1920 and worked at San Joaquin Light and Power as a clerk and cashier.

Peirson Ancestry

The spelling of "Peirson" is not common. The basis for the name comes from the shores of Normandy in France where the son of Pierre's surname would be "Pierson". This name showed up in England in the 15th Century.

The "Peirson" variation of the name began to show up as "e" before "i" which is a common spelling order in England and oftentimes it was based on how the local church would record someone's name as many were illiterate.

Three brothers: Thomas, Abraham, and Henry Peirson emigrated to America from Olney, England in 1639 to Boston. Abraham's son, Abraham Pierson, Jr. ("i" before "e" altered spelling) would become the first president of Yale.

Henry Peirson settled in Long Island, NY and married Mary Cooper in 1642. Around 1780, three of their great, great grandsons, Nathan, Zachariah and Jeremiah, moved to Richmond. Zachariah married Sarah Sandford.

Wilfred Robinson Peirson

1896 Wilfred as child; 1917 WW1 Uniform; 1918 in French bar

Wilfred Robinson Peirson was born on November 5, 1893, in Holder, Illinois to John James and Anna Katherine (Saams) Peirson. Zacharia and Sarah Peirson's great, great grandson, John James Peirson was Wilfred's father.

He was the second youngest of five brothers and sisters. His other siblings were Nellie (1884), Bessie (1887), Elmer (1888 who died as an infant), Henry (1891) and Lucile (1896).

When Wilfred was around 18 years old, his father offered to send him to college, but he decided to work for the railroad, as he thought it would make more money. He later changed his mind and went to his father and asked if the college offer was still available. His father told him that he had his chance and now it was gone. He ended up taking odd jobs as a mechanic and learned the air conditioning and heating trade in later years.

In December 1917, at the age of 24, he joined the Army in the midst of World War One. A few months later he was deployed to France.

Wilfred was assigned to the 13 company, 3rd Regional Air Service and served as a mechanic for flying ace Captain Eddie Rickenbacker. The war ended in November 1918 and he was honorably discharged from the Army Air Service in July 1919.

In 1919, Wilfred worked for Buick in Murphysboro, Illinois, as an auto mechanic. He took some college classes that same year at the University of Illinois, Champagne, before moving to Detroit, Michigan in October 1919 and got a job at U.S. Rubber Company as a tire finisher.

Erma and Wilfred Peirson

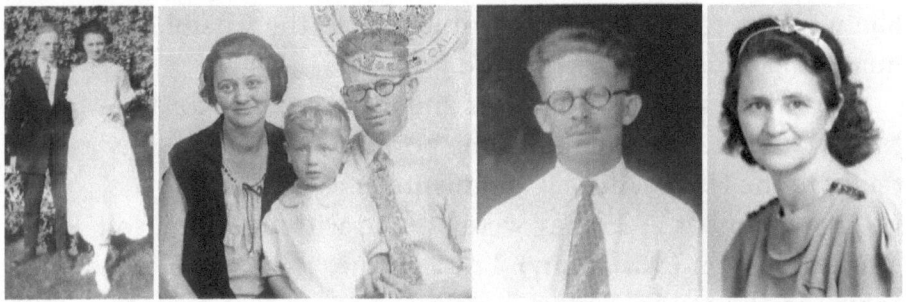

Marriage in 1922; Passport from 1928 for their move to Columbia; Wilfred Peirson and Erma Peirson portraits from 1930s

Wilfred Peirson met Erma Patterson in Walnut Creek, CA in 1921 where they were both living. It was a tough economic time as it was a depression in the early 1920s known as the "Forgotten Depression" that preceded "The Great Depression".

They were married on September 3, 1922, in Walnut Creek, CA. Wilfred was 28 and Erma 31 years old at the time. Wilfred continued his job with the County Farm Bureau and Erma started a job as a billing clerk at the Sugar Pine Lumber Company in Madera.

Shortly after their marriage, Wilfred found an unimproved 20-acre tract five miles outside Madera. The plot had been part of a large grain ranch. The only structure on it was a massive, pigeon-infested barn. They bought it and planned to harvest fig and apricot trees, plant gardens and raise chickens on their little California Ranch which they called the Bide A Wee Ranch.

Wilfred drew up plans for a compact, convenient little dwelling of three rooms, a bathroom, and screened-in porch. He hired a local retired carpenter who was a friend of the family, and they built the little house in two months.

Erma's job at the lumber company allowed her the privilege of purchasing building materials at cost. The house was equipped with coal oil lamps and was later wired for electricity. While living there, they had one of the earliest radios to listen to the nighttime news and programs using an earphone.

In 1923, Erma's job ended when the former billing clerk returned. She went on to work two part-time jobs at the Chamber of Commerce and Gibbs Hardware Store.

For a year she was a reporter and feature writer for the Madera Mercury news. She got a full-time position with the County as Secretary to the Horticultural Commissioner.

In September 1925 they were blessed with their first son, James Marlow Peirson (aka Jimmy). Erma left her job to care for the new baby and the ranch. Unfortunately, the ranch was struggling with high water costs and alkali soil issues causing the trees to suffer blight. On top of that, the effects of the depression reduced Wilfred's pay, dramatically.

In February of 1926, they walked away from their dream home in order to find a better income. The small family of three moved to Oakland, CA where Wilfred got a job as a cashier at National Ice Cream. The following year, they moved to Yuba City where he got a clerical job for California Petroleum. In 1928, he got another job as a tire inspector in Montebello, CA.

Because Wilfred had difficulty staying gainfully employed due to the economic depression, he decided to move their little family to

Extended Biography

Colombia, South America in September of 1928 for a job there in the Oil Industry.

At one point during their voyage, Jimmy was in a stroller on the ship's deck with Wilfred. He decided to move them inside and moments after they left the spot where Jimmy's stroller had been sitting, a large piece of the ship's hoisting gear came crashing down. Little Jimmy dodged certain death that day.

The family resided in Barrancabermeja, Colombia and during his time there, Wilfred gained a working knowledge of Spanish. He worked for the Tropical Oil Company as an Assistant Cashier and Paymaster. His employment included a furnished house and paid utilities.

In November 1928 they had a daughter and named her Doris Mae Peirson. They were expecting their third child when they decided to return to America in December 1929. When they arrived in Los Angeles, there was concern about the pregnancy and Erma was put on bed rest.

Wilfred (aka Billy) Saams Peirson was born in Artesia, California in May 1930.

Upon their return to America, Wilfred got a job as an automobile salesman in Bellflower, CA for Cameron Chevrolet for about 6 months. Shortly after Billy was born, he got a new job at Husband & Seed as an accountant.

In May 1932, Wilfred went out on his own and was the owner/operator of "Malted Milk Shop and Fountain Lunch" in the Spurgeon Building in Santa Ana, CA. In September 1933, his business failed due to the Great Depression. The original building is still there, and a coffee shop is in its place.

During the early 1930s, Wilfred was doing odd jobs, so the family moved from town to town and house to house. They would occupy a place for the first month and when the rent came due, they would simply move on to another place.

In April 1934, Wilfred got a job at Kelvinator, installing and servicing refrigeration and air conditioning units.

Looking for a better opportunity, Wilfred left Kelvinator and moved the family to Salt Lake City, Utah in July 1936 for a job as an Appliance Installation and Service Manager at the Flint Distribution Company. They were there for 16 months.

Although her main focus was on raising their three children, Erma enjoyed writing. She even had articles published in *Boys' Life* and *Progress* magazines.

In April 1941, while living in Riverside, CA, Wilfred had surgery on his colon. He spent three months recovering at Veterans Hospital in Sawtelle, CA. He got a government job in July 1941 and commuted to Barstow from Riverside, being home on weekends, until the family followed in 1943.

Wilfred worked for the US Army at Camp Irwin as a mechanical engineer. Erma also got jobs for the war effort at Yermo Holding Reconsignment Point and in the public relations office at Daggett airfield.

It was while living in Barstow that Erma developed a love for the desert. She would travel up and down the communities and towns along the Mojave River and talk to the older people who lived there to document their stories about the area and the river.

In 1945 the family moved to China Lake, CA when Wilfred got a job at the naval base as a Mechanical Engineer and then as an Assistant Building Engineer at Michelson Laboratory. He oversaw all refrigeration and air conditioning on the base.

The couple were active in several organizations, particularly in Veterans and Masonic groups. Wilfred was affiliated with the Indian Wells Valley Lions Club. Erma was a charter member and the first chaplain of the Desert Holly Chapter, Order of Eastern Star. In 1951, she served as Worthy Matron.

Erma worked as associate editor and then editor of the *Rocketeer* from 1945 to 1950. While there, she wrote a column called "Desert Spotlight" with personal notes of people of the community. She then began writing a weekly series under the title of "Desert Scrapbook" which grew into a collection of 220 desert articles in the *Rocketeer*.

She also contributed 23 articles in a series called "Death Valley Lore" for the *Ridgecrest Herald.*

Erma attributes her direction to write a desert book to desert author Major George Palmer Putman, the husband of Amelia Earhart. He had remarried after her death and was living in Mount Whitney Portals, north of China Lake. She had an interview with him for the *Rocketeer* and he discovered her interest in the desert. He told her, "Mrs. Peirson, promise me something. Stay with the desert. You write so well."

In 1956, Erma wrote *The Kern's Desert*, which was published by the Kern County Historical Society. It was the first book she officially published and was well received.

For many years, Wilfred suffered from hardening of the arteries in his legs. During experimental surgery for it, blood flow to his right leg was blocked too long, so they had to amputate it. They gave him a wooden leg, and he used crutches to get around. He loved his eight grandchildren who called him Bapa and would let them sit on his wooden leg and knock on it. Their older grandchildren vividly remember him giving them rides on that leg.

Because of losing his leg, Wilfred was unable to continue his job at the naval base and retired in 1957. One of the gifts he got upon his retirement was a desert painting by famed local artist Edward Hammerberg of China Lake. Since they lived in base housing, they were forced to move. They relocated to Fresno that same year.

Erma enrolled in the local college in the fall of 1957 and at the age of 67, she had the distinction of being the oldest member of the graduating class of 1958 when she received her degree in General Education at Fresno City College. Most of her credits were transfers from attending the University of California seminar program while living in China Lake.

One distinction Erma had was being a member of the Fresno County Historical Society. In 1959, she even became a member of the Board of Directors.

Wilfred died from a stroke on August 7, 1963. Officers of the Ponderosa Masonic Lodge conducted the funeral services, and he was interred at Belmont Memorial Park in Fresno.

Erma Peirson

Erma with grandchildren in 1964; Erma portrait; Sisters Ruby and Erma in 1968

From July 1963 until January 1965, she wrote a column called "Fresno's Past" in the *Fresno Guide* newspaper. It ran every Thursday for 78 weeks.

Erma moved to Apple Valley and became the editor of the *Apple Valley Bonanza* and wrote weekly articles. She had one series called "Apple Valley Golden Land". She also wrote a column for the *Hesperia Resorter* called "Desert Drama".

She published her book *The Mojave River and Its Valley* in 1970. It may still be in some libraries today. It was highly regarded and was her life's work.

One interesting fact she found during research for the book was that sometimes people coming through California where the Mojave River was located would die of thirst, as they thought there was no water available since it appeared as though the river was dry. Little did they know that most of the time that river runs underground. Few realized that 18 inches below the riverbed, water was running through it that could have saved their lives.

The town of Apple Valley declared July 31, 1970, as "Erma Peirson Day", in recognition of her efforts and her love for the desert.

Erma passed away July 21, 1971 at the age of 80, following a heart attack. At that point she had 12 grandchildren to carry on her legacy. Her eldest grandchild, Trisha, was responsible for awarding Erma the nick name of "Marnie". She was unable to pronounce "Grandma" properly and that was how it came out. It stuck and was a moniker Erma enjoyed.

She is interred next to Wilfred at Belmont Memorial Park in Fresno. Her nickname was even included on her tombstone.

At the time of her passing, she was working on her third book that was going to cover the history of Fresno drawn from her newspaper column by the same name, which was published posthumously in 2024, entitled *Fresno's Past*.

James Marlow Peirson

Jim in 1932; Air Reservist 1944; Medical School 1949

James (Jim) was born on September 5, 1925, in Madera, CA. His early adult years were spent in San Jose, CA and other areas in Northern California.

In his teen years, the family lived in Riverside, CA where he graduated from Riverside Polytechnic High School in 1943. He applied to West Point but never attended. He was in the Army Air Service as World War II was in full swing. By the time he got his orders to go overseas, the war was coming to an end, so he never left the country.

Wilfred, his father, wanted him to be an engineer, so he followed his father's guidance and attended college as an engineering major in Fresno. However, he really wanted to be a doctor, so after a few years he changed his studies to medicine and got his medical degree at the Los Angeles Osteopath Physicians and Surgeons, later to become part of UC Irvine Medical School.

Jim met his future wife through his sister, Doris, who was a teacher in Trona. Claire Huppert was a friend of Doris' and a fellow teacher at the same school. On August 14, 1953, Jim and Claire were married and moved to Bell, CA.

A few years later they followed his family roots and moved to Illinois. He needed a state license to practice medicine, so he enrolled in classes there. During that time, he worked at a winery on an assembly line bottling the wine.

Claire's asthma did not handle the climate well, so they moved back to California before he got a chance to get his medical license. For a short period of time, they lived in Fresno before moving to Southern California, eventually settling in Cypress in Orange County.

He had a photographic memory. His hobbies included the ham radio and photography. Jim and Claire had four children, Wilafred, James, Joseph and Melinda.

Jim passed away in 2002.

Doris Mae (Peirson) Dye

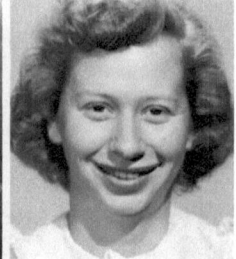

Young Doris with big brother Jim in 1932; Doris with dog; Burroughs High School, Class of 1946

Doris was born in Barrancabermeja, Columbia, South America, on November 7, 1928, when the family lived there because of a job venture their father took. They returned to California in 1930, shortly before the new addition of her little brother, Billy, was born.

She was a member of the first graduating class at Burroughs High School in 1946. She was editor of the first yearbook, first queen of the prom and a cheerleader.

Following her graduation, she attended Whittier College, University of Nevada, Las Vegas and Fresno State College. She received her teaching credential from Chapman College. Her first teaching roles were in schools near Fresno. Doris returned to Indian Wells Valley to teach in Trona, CA.

On September 4, 1954, she married Charles (Chuck) M. Dye Jr in China Lake, CA where he worked as a nuclear physicist. They had five children, Patricia, Wendy, Richard, Michael and Charles Jr.

After raising her children in Ridgecrest, CA, she returned to teaching at Las Flores Elementary School and then moved to Theodore H. Faller Elementary School, where she remained for 15 years. At Faller, she began her musical programs, enhancing her students and her career. She touched many students' lives, as evidenced by the number of letters she received upon her retirement.

Doris' second love was the game of bridge. She was an American Contact Bridge League Life Master. She actively managed a local bridge club and taught bridge classes.

Doris passed away in 2004.

Wilfred Saams Peirson

Young Bill with Doris and Jim in La Habra in front of Uncle Henry's car in 1932; Bill with rooster in Barstow 1943; Bill at Fort Hood, TX in 1948.

Wilfred (Bill) was born on May 19, 1930, in Artesia, CA. He was the youngest of his siblings Jim and Doris. He went by the name "Billy" during his childhood.

Bill grew up during the Great Depression and his family moved around a lot. They lived in the Riverside, CA area in his pre-teen years where he was involved in the YMCA. In 1942, that they relocated to Barstow, CA, where he attended 7th and 8th grades.

They finally settled down in 1945 in China Lake, CA. Bill attended Burroughs High School in nearby Ridgecrest and was active in many sports and the student council. He was a popular student, known as "Burro Bill." He graduated in 1948.

Bill worked briefly for the US Postal Service before joining the Army in July 1948. He did not want to get drafted and figured if he enlisted, he would have better options. He served a one-year enlistment at Fort Hood in Texas then returned to the postal service.

In 1950, Bill got called up to the Army due to the Korean War. He was almost shipped off to the front lines where two-thirds of his infantry died in battle.

The reason it didn't happen had to do with the spelling of his name. As he stood in line waiting to be deployed, they pointed to him and said, "That man has been scratched". He was left standing alone as he watched everyone get loaded onto trucks to eventually be put onto planes embarking for Korea. Eventually, a truck picked him up and took him back to the barracks, where he sat all alone. He had an idea what was going on and chose to keep his mouth shut and simply wait to find out. Finally, his Sargent came to see him and told him they had lost his medical records. His medical records were filed as "Pierson" instead of "Peirson".

He was finally deployed to Korea on December 7, 1950 with another batch of soldiers in the Army surveying crew for artillery operations. He was a forward observer directing artillery shells which was a dangerous role as the enemy knew if they got the observer, the artillery shots would stop until a new person took over. He also had to run communication wires prior to battle.

In February of 1951, he got pneumonia because it was winter, and he only had his summer government issue clothing. He had to be evacuated to a M.A.S.H unit and later to a hospital in Osaka, Japan for four months where he contracted tuberculous. He was sent to Japan to recuperate and to a sanitarium in Duarte, CA for nine months to recover. He was bored there as he was told to rest and no activity. They eventually got him a radio, and he would read the Los Angeles Times every day.

He attended Fresno State and later transferred to UC Berkeley and graduated in 1957 with a Bachelor of Science Degree in Civil Engineering. He got his first professional job at Granite Construction Company. He did not like it there as it was a big company with lots of rules about when you could take breaks and what you worked on. Bill worked for small construction firms in Berkeley, CA and Oakland, CA until he married Donna Marie Harris on June 18, 1960.

Bill and Donna had three children, Robert, Susan and Julie. Bill continued to work jobs at multiple small construction firms bouncing between Fresno, CA and Victorville, CA.

In 1969, he moved his family briefly to Australia to work on as a civil engineering. The lifestyle was much different than in the USA, so they returned later in the year. They traveled both ways by Ocean Liner.

By 1975, they had permanently settled in the Mojave High Desert including Apple Valley and Hesperia. He built their 5,000 square foot dream home in Hesperia overlooking the golf course and enjoyed his retirement years there.

Bill passed away in 2016.

Exhibit – Ancestry Tree

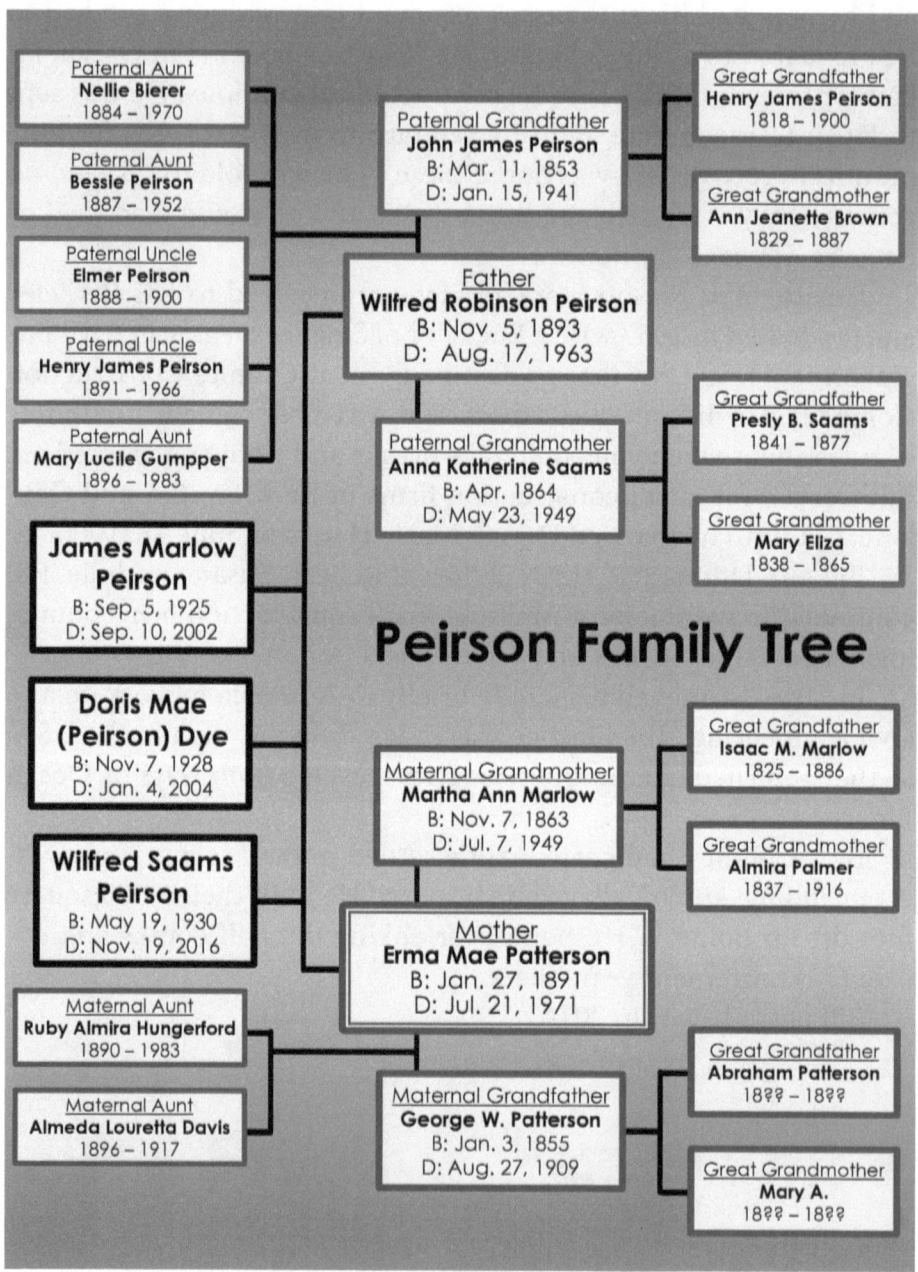

www.ingramcontent.com/pod-product-compliance
Lightning Source LLC
Chambersburg PA
CBHW030454100526
44580CB00010B/126/J